THE
GEN-SAVVY
FINANCIAL
ADVISOR

Advising the Generations in
the New Age of Uncertainty

CAM MARSTON

The Gen-Savvy Financial Advisor: Advising the Generations in the New Age of Uncertainty

Copyright © 2017 by Generational Insights. All Rights Reserved.

For information about this title or to order other books and/or electronic media, contact the publisher:
Generational Insights
PO Box 81118
Mobile, AL 36689
www.generationalinsights.com
info@generationalinsights.com

Library of Congress Control Number: 2016920669

ISBN: 978-0-9982627-0-3 (print)
       978-0-9982627-1-0 (eBook)

Printed in the United States of America

Cover and Interior design: 1106 Design

Acknowledgements

Acknowledgements for this revised edition must begin with two people: Megan Merchant and Gerald Bierling.

Megan has, once again, taken my amorphous direction of "it needs to be updated to reflect the changes since the first version" and helped me produce a book I'm very proud of. She's always quick with ideas that solve the problems we encounter, and just as importantly, keeps me in check when my ideas run amok. She continues to be a delight to work with. Simply put: Megan is the bomb.

Gerald is also a delight. He seeks out the data I need to support the arguments I make and has never returned empty-handed. He offers insight and different interpretations of information that I would never have considered without him. Always eager to dig deeper, Gerald has become a key resource for the development and credibility of my work.

A nod must go out to my office team: Helen Broder and Susan Poliquin. Both of them keep me moving in the right direction with clients, conference calls, contracts, and travel. I'd be a failure at my work if it weren't for them.

I must mention Steven James since his work is largely responsible for the first edition of *The Gen-Savvy Financial Advisor.* The first edition did not have an acknowledgement section, and this recognition is long overdue.

Many financial services companies have been generous with their attention, their feedback, and their support of my research. The list is too long to print here, but they know who they are, and it is always a treat to reconnect with them.

Finally, I must mention my wife and kids. They support my work and my exhaustive travel, and they let me back in when I come home, eager to greet me with smiles on their faces. Leaving is hard. Coming home is a thrill. But I can't have one without the other.

TABLE OF CONTENTS

**Chapter 1   Generational Differences and
Financial Advising**. 1
The Generations 4
Generation-Savvy Financial Advising. 5

Chapter 2   Advising Matures. 7
The Matures 7
Three Reasons Mature Clients Matter 8
Four Classic Mature Client Characteristics. 10
Three Financial Traits of Mature Clients 12
Eight Ways to Connect with Mature Clients. 14
Four Key Advisor Questions for Working
   with Matures 21

Chapter 3   Advising Baby Boomers 23
The Baby Boomers. 23
Three Reasons Baby Boomer Clients Matter. 24
Ten Classic Boomer Client Characteristics. 26
Seven Financial Traits of Baby Boomers 31

Fourteen Ways to Connect with Baby
   Boomer Clients................................ 40
BOOMERS AND THEIR CHILDREN................ 57
Six Key Advisor Questions for Preparing to
   Work with Boomers 59

Chapter 4 Advising Generation X **61**
The Xers... 61
Four Reasons Gen X Clients Matter 62
Eleven Classic Gen X Client Attitudes
   and Characteristics...........................65
Seven Financial Traits of Generation X...........75
Fifteen Ways to Connect with Gen X Clients 82
THE MARRIED GEN X MOTHER..................98
Seven Key Advisor Questions for Preparing
   to Work with Generation X 100

Chapter 5 Advising Millennials....................**103**
The Millennials..................................103
Five Reasons Millennial Clients Matter 105
Fifteen Classic Millennial Client Attitudes
   and Characteristics...........................108
Millennial Caveat................................ 119
Eight Financial Traits of Millennials 121
Fifteen Ways to Connect with
   Millennial Clients............................ 131
GEN X, MILLENNIALS, AND SOCIAL MEDIA...... 144
Five Key Advisor Questions for Preparing
   to Work with Millennials 148

Chapter 6 The Generational Transition **151**

   The Great Transfer............................ 151

   An Existential Threat or Once-in-a-Lifetime

      Opportunity................................152

   Case Study: "Michael and Jennifer".............153

   Case Study: "Dave"...........................155

   Case Study: "Jim and Earl".....................156

   Twelve Steps to Manage Generational

      Transition 163

Conclusion **169**

About the Author **171**

Resources **175**

Foreword

For decades, financial services have focused on target markets that approached investment and financial services through traditional and customary advisor-client relationships. Buying habits have shifted significantly in recent years, including the way individuals buy financial services. Generation X and Millennials have different economic and cultural experiences from their Baby Boomer and Mature parents and grandparents, and are now squarely in the age ranges that make them prime markets for investments, retirement planning, and other financial services.

This change in target audience demographics is producing shockwaves and aftershocks that will shake the financial services industry. This guide provides an in-depth overview of the generations and their approaches to finance, as well as some clear guidelines and techniques for engaging with your changing clientele.

The challenge for financial advisors is to provide financial services and create new advisor-client relationships that match the expectations and experiences of the new generations of investors. The Great Recession and its aftermath altered the financial outlook for every generation in a different way, creating additional challenges for you as an advisor. New generational attitudes have surfaced in response to new realities. In addition to understanding each generation's characteristics, advisors should also understand their distinct anxieties and concerns, which have been prompted by the downturn and recovery.

Above all, advisors need to understand and embrace the need to reach out to new generations of clients. Here are just a few startling facts that reflect the coming changes in the marketplace for investment advice and financial planning:

- The 40 to 59 year-old demographic among potential clients will grow by 2.6% between 2016 and 2026, and 5.1% between 2026 and 2036.

- 37% of wealthy investors (those with at least $3 million in investible assets) are between 18 and 51 years old; 42% are Baby Boomers (ages 52–70).

- Investors between 23 and 55 will inherit more than $41 trillion in assets by 2052.

- 66% of children "fire" their parents' financial advisor after they inherit their parents' wealth. (Some reports suggest this number is actually much higher.)

- 39% of Millennials say they've never interacted with their parents' financial advisors; only 11% indicate that they already work with their parents' advisors.

Chapter 1

Generational Differences and Financial Advising

A major factor in building successful client relationships is the likability factor: one's capacity to establish a connection or rapport consistently with prospects and clients. Clients need to be comfortable with a person before trusting them with investment and financial decisions. That comfort level is expressed in phrases like, "He gets me," or "She just knows exactly where I'm coming from," or, if you're really lucky, "Hey, I *like* this guy!"

Sometimes, establishing this connection is easy. You can simply hit it off with a client, especially one with whom you share a common background, age group, or interest. Other times, however, the connection seems more difficult. Sometimes, you can't seem to find the right "wavelength", or you feel that you aren't speaking the same language. This likely happens most often with clients and prospects of different ages and backgrounds than your own. You haven't shared similar experiences, so you have a different perspective of the world. This is often due to unconscious generational bias.

Everyone sees the world through his or her own generational filter. Age and life stages also dictate many needs and preferences. In some cases, the differences between generations are minor, while other differences may prevent the formation of an advisor-client relationship. Many of the things that help advisors "get" clients come with the ability to understand clients' generational points of view. Often, the failure to connect with a client—to understand where he or she is coming from—lies in an inability to tap into a common generational background.

For example, older and younger generations have fundamentally different views of financial markets. Older generations, Matures and Boomers, have basic confidence that the principles of the market will continue to apply—that the market will eventually reward sound investing in spite of the occasional ups and downs, despite many having had their investments hit right at the time they needed to use those funds. Younger generations, on the other hand, look at recent ups and downs and see a financial marketplace that is risky and unstable. They are convinced things are different now. The market of their parents and grandparents is gone, they believe. They lack that sense of continuity and confidence that guided so many generations back to the market after downturns past. And, frankly, the younger generations simply distrust the financial services marketplace. Their point of view is that the Great Recession was evidence that the system is rigged against them. So today's advisor is fighting an uphill battle simply to gain their trust in the system, and that's no easy task.

Understanding clients' age-based points of view is an indispensable soft skill that you can use to establish connections and make sales. While no one can be all things to all people, earning a little likability will help a financial advisor build the trust necessary for an advising relationship. Likeability helps you connect quickly with clients, get them to listen to what you have to say, start a relationship with you, and continue to build it. All of this, of course, contributes to your ability to provide better financial advice because you will have a better sense of the clients' true goals and the biases that may be holding them back.

THE GENERATIONS

Today, there are four distinct generations in the market for financial advising. Each of these generations has shared experiences and characteristics, and each presents distinct challenges and opportunities to financial professionals. Of course, generational biases are not ironclad, and birth date does not dictate personality. Naturally, financial advisors must first develop a thorough knowledge of the products and services they offer, an understanding of their industry's competitive landscape, and a solid grasp of advising principles. But even well-equipped account advisors can be handicapped by a lack of generational insight.

Here's a quick comparison of the four generations with whom you'll need to be able to form strong relationships, and some of the shared experiences that have defined their collective generational biases:

Name	Birth Years	Size¹	Age in 2016	Defining Moments
Matures	1945 and prior	31.7 million	70-plus	• Great Depression • World War II • Hiroshima • GI Bill
Baby Boomers	1946 to 1964	74.9 million	52 to 70	• Civil Rights • Kennedy and King assassinations • Vietnam War • Woodstock
Generation X	1965 to 1979	61.5 million	37 to 51	• Challenger explosion • Watergate • Clinton sex scandal • PC boom
Millennials	1980 to 2000	92.3 million	16 to 36	• 9/11 attacks • Connected via tech—always on • Social media boom • Baby on Board

¹2015 U.S. Census Bureau

GENERATION-SAVVY FINANCIAL ADVISING

While it's usually easy to communicate with members of your own generation, it's also easy to get signals crossed when communicating cross-generationally. Sending the wrong generational signals can significantly alienate clients. Approaches that work with older generations may identify you as "like my parents" for younger customers. Members of a different age group might perceive methods of communication that seem normal to you as intrusive. Such potential generation gaps in the relationship between you and your clients could cost you an account.

In addition, each generation has a different investing and financial outlook, according to their life and career stages. Likewise, each has different attitudes toward different financial instruments, strategies, products, and means of investment, planning, and saving. Each generation has felt a different kind of impact from the Great Recession. Some generations are leery of traditional financial instruments. Some feel safer with the tried-and-true. Some generations are innately distrustful of financial services. Others instinctively trust them.

The following chapters will help you explore these differences so that you can become a generation-savvy advisor who is able to establish cross-generational relationships with the clientele who will sustain you and your practice for the next half-century.

CHAPTER 2

ADVISING MATURES

THE MATURES

The Matures should be well known to most advisors today. They are seniors (born prior to 1945) who either fought in World War II or were children during the war. Some experienced the Great Depression in addition to the Great Recession. In fact, many of their current behaviors can be traced back to the depression—whether due to their own experiences or the effects it had on their parents. The Matures are defined by a deep understanding of sacrifice and scarcity, stemming from these two major American experiences.

THREE REASONS MATURE CLIENTS MATTER

1. **Small but mighty.** Today, the Matures number just under 32 million, or less than 10% of the population. But due to their upbringing, most Matures are quite frugal. By applying that frugality to an economic boom during their peak earning years, many Matures have amassed a solid portfolio of financial assets. Their collective net worth is declining as many live longer than they had perhaps planned for financially; however, on average, their net worth in 2013 slightly outpaced that of the Boomers. The Boomers maintain greater economic power because of their vast numbers and more consumer-oriented nature.

2. **Loyal and steadfast.** Matures are the most patriotic generation, having been asked to sacrifice for our country and having had that sacrifice respected by the nation and returned in the form of programs such as the GI Bill. They are also the last generation to experience company loyalty. By and large, they worked for the same company their entire careers

and are similarly consistent in the way they do business. If you treat a Mature client well, you have a client for life.

3. **Unsustainable.** It is highly unlikely a member of the Mature generation will be searching for a new financial advisor at this point in life. Unless their current relationships fail, they won't see the need for help and will stay with what they know. But those who you are already working with are likely a significant portion of your firm's portfolio. If you do not have a plan to manage the transition of wealth to the next generation, this is a problem. The Mature population will fall by more than 50% by 2026. Understanding how that change will affect your business is imperative.

FOUR CLASSIC MATURE CLIENT CHARACTERISTICS

1. **Rule followers.** Matures came of age during a time when the military was a significant influence. Rules were important. As children and as adults, Matures understood that you did what was expected of you and you knew what to expect as a result. This worldview translates into their expectations of others.

2. **Hierarchy matters.** As rule followers, Matures also understand and respect a chain of command. Borrowing again from the military influence, that chain of command—and therefore deference and authority—is determined by place, not necessarily by action. Members of the Mature generation will expect respect simply because of their life experiences.

3. **Patriots.** You may be noticing a theme here. Law, order, respect for authority, and sacrifice. These are all hallmarks of the Mature generation. They lived through vast changes

in American society and are proud of what this country endured and overcame.

4. **Body, mind, and spirit may not be in sync.** The youngest Matures are in their early 70s, and Al Roker celebrates the oldest on the *Today* show. Unfortunately, while Americans are living longer, they are dealing with more health needs than ever before. According to a Census Bureau report, nearly 35% of Matures are disabled in some way, and almost 50% state that their health is fair or poor.

THREE FINANCIAL TRAITS OF MATURE CLIENTS

1. **Deep in retirement.** Only 11% of Matures are still in the workforce, and only 9% of retired Matures still work in any capacity. Matures largely approached retirement as an end game; they expected to stop working or lessen their workload at a certain age, and by and large, they did. Despite their collective affluence, however, many have concerns about outliving their savings and investments—especially when considering the long-term care needs that come with declining health.

2. **Underplanned but okay.** More than half of Matures do not meet with a financial advisor (although 1 in 5 does meet with an advisor at least once a year). However, 60% have a budget or plan for how they will spend their retirement funds. While roughly half of the Matures feel their expenses in retirement are on par with their expectations, 42% are finding expenses somewhat or much higher than expected. Most still feel that they are living comfortably or doing okay financially,

and that their financial status hasn't changed drastically in the last 12 months.

3. **Willing to listen.** Compared to other generations, Matures are among the most willing to seek out professional financial advice. Almost half of respondents to a U.S. Federal Reserve Board survey on household economics stated that they relied on financial planners (30%), investment brokers (11%), lawyers, or accountants for financial advice. The data does not offer reasons, but based on this generation's belief in hierarchy and trust in authority, seeking out expert opinions makes sense.

EIGHT WAYS TO CONNECT WITH MATURE CLIENTS

1. **Know the rules.** Matures expect order and may have an internal list of their "rules of engagement." You can't be expected to know precisely what those rules are, but you will be expected to follow them. So ask up front.

    Try this: "What do I need to know to provide you with the best service?"

    Or: "What do I need to know about working with you so that you get what you need from this relationship? Any past experiences—good or bad—that I can learn from?"

2. **Don't patronize.** This is certainly a good rule for all generations, but it is particularly important when speaking about Matures. Painting this generation with a broad brush and assuming that they are less current or contemporary may seem easy; however, do not assume that being retired means they are

disengaged from the world. Take care not to make assumptions about what they may or may not know or care about. Be careful not to make assumptions that will make them feel stupid or embarrassed.

> *Try this:* "I've been looking at (news/ current event) and thinking about how it applies to your investments. I'd recommend…"
>
> *Or:* "Have you been following the developments in the European Union? While your investments are primarily in low-risk areas, we continue to monitor the global economy."

3. **Show deference.** As mentioned above, Matures believe in hierarchy and authority. They have earned respect through their experiences and, of course, in their position as the client. Regardless of your age, use formal titles with this generation unless you are asked or invited to do otherwise. This

may be especially hard for Gen X advisors, who may be inclined to treat everyone as their equal.

   Try this: "Yes, ma'am" and "No, sir"— it's really as simple as that.

4. **Demonstrate patriotism.** Patriotism is a kissing cousin to politics, so you need to be careful here, but it can help build connection points with Matures. Anything that helps establish a connection and comfort can help build the trust and interpersonal relationships that matter in financial advising. Do not make a big production of your patriotism; simply incorporate subtle, honest touches that speak to your love of country.

   Try this: If you served in the military, display your honors in the office.

   Or: Fly the flag properly at your place of business and wear a lapel pin.

5. **Make them comfortable.** As with any generation, Matures face increasing health concerns as they age. And as you would expect,

they don't necessarily want to talk about it. But they do want to be able to move comfortably through the world. Consider the needs of this client base in the way you set up your reception and meeting areas. Make sure chairs are wide and have sturdy arms to assist with standing or sitting. If you are meeting outside of the office, consider the setting and minimize the potential for noise that will make it difficult to hear.

> *Try this:* If you know a client will be in a wheelchair, arrange the table so that they can pull straight up to an existing space at the table. Also, be careful of throw rugs that may become trip or slip hazards. Remove them when your clients come to visit.

> *Or this:* Get rid of cheap stick pens and invest in wide-barrel, comfort-grip pens to make signing documents easier for clients with arthritis.

6. **Welcome their children.** The children of the Matures, comprised of both Baby Boomers

and Gen Xers, can be expected to be involved with their parents' finances to some degree. Whether through physical care (transporting to/from meetings), as part of the planning strategy of inheritances and long-term care, or through power of attorney, they most likely have a role. When meeting with multiple generations at once, you'll need to understand the biases of each as well as their personal roles in the meeting. Remember, too, who the primary client is, regardless of who has the strongest voice. See page 52 for more specifics on working with clients' adult children.

> ⠿ *Try this:* "It's nice to see so that you have so much support. Let me know what type of information you'd like me to share with your family, and I'll be happy to do so."

7. **Test out technology.** Having lived most of their lives without the internet and mobile technology, Matures are usually not early adopters of new technology. They are, however, surprisingly fast adopters of established

technology. They don't embrace e-commerce with the fervor of Millennials or Gen Xers, and are even less likely to engage in online financial services, but they do use online media socially and recreationally.

> ·💡· *Try this:* "Do you follow our firm's Facebook page? I often share bits of information there that I think clients find helpful or interesting."

> *Or this:* "We are happy to send you a reminder prior to our next meeting. Would you prefer to get that as a phone call, email or text?"

8. **Prepare for memory loss.** Age-related dementia is becoming more prevalent as life expectancies increase. Nobody wants to deal with it, but it is incredibly important that you pay attention and introduce contingencies early so that your clients' interests are fulfilled— even if they become unable to make financial decisions themselves. Be aware that these important aspects of aging are incredibly delicate to discuss. The AARP has excellent

resources for working with this generation, particularly as it relates to dementia and loss of memory and the legal tangles that you'll need to be aware of.

FOUR KEY ADVISOR QUESTIONS FOR WORKING WITH MATURES

Ask yourself:

1. How do my own generational biases conflict with those of the Matures? Where might this create unintentional discomfort?

2. What can I do to develop relationships with the children of my Mature clients? Are my clients interested in participating in a formal family discussion, facilitated by me? Consider hosting information sessions with guest speakers on topics related to aging parents and caregiving.

3. Where can I build relationships that will help my clients make the connections they need beyond financial services? Lawyers, long-term care, etc.? Matures are likely to trust these referrals and will appreciate vetted connections.

4. Is my office physically comfortable for clients with disabilities? Is the office a welcoming environment both in how we treat clients and in the physical layout?

Chapter 3

Advising Baby Boomers

The Baby Boomers

The Baby Boomers are the wealthiest generation of consumers in American history. They are just under a quarter of the population, but they account for over half of consumer spending. Many Boomers are in senior leadership and management positions at work, and most are in their earning peak. Yet, 25% have already retired. Many still have dependent children, whether school age or adult. They are known for their work ethic, and they like to reward themselves for all of that hard work with the best things in life. They feel they deserve it.

Three Reasons Baby Boomer Clients Matter

1. **Size.** They number nearly 75 million. Because of this generation's size, they will continue to redefine each stage of life they pass through. For example, they have become the largest market ever for products and services related to aging and retirement.

2. **Wealth.** It is estimated that Baby Boomers control 50% of net household wealth across the U.S. and have over $2 trillion in annual spending power, a staggering figure. Simply put, they have more money to spend than any generation in human history. The Great Recession put a dent in their wealth, but if their investments were in the stock market, then their wealth has probably exceeded that of 2007 due to its rebound. The recession did dampen their spirits slightly, with 1 in 5, feeling like they are "just getting by" according to a recent Transamerica survey.

3. **They are in transition.** Many Boomers are already in retirement, but many more are near the end of their careers, transitioning toward retirement. Many will be adjusting their lifestyles, moving, buying second homes, or downsizing as they pack their kids off to college, search for retirement destinations, and look for a place to park their considerable investments and savings.

There is also a transition within the Boomer ranks with Leading Boomers (born 1946–1955) and Trailing Boomers (born 1956–1964) having different outlooks on retirement expectations (for example, Trailing Boomers expect to work longer and get less retirement help from anyone other than themselves). Despite the massive wealth of this generation, neither Leading nor Trailing Boomers feel quite confident in their financial readiness.

TEN CLASSIC BOOMER CLIENT CHARACTERISTICS

1. **Competitive.** The Baby Boomers are a very competitive generation; they were competitive in the workplace and will remain so in retirement. With so many Boomers around, competition between them has always been fierce, and their experience has taught them that those who compete the hardest usually win. They have often perfected the art of "keeping up with the Joneses" and surpassing them. They often like to have something that's just a little bit better than what everyone else has. For most of their careers, Boomers worked hard for the awards and trophies that adorn their walls. As they near or experience retirement, however, they are beginning to place more value on time and experiences.

2. **Optimistic and idealistic.** From their youth, Boomers retain the sense that things can and will keep getting better. Their experiences are that if they work hard and pursue the

right goals, they will be rewarded. Boomers still carry with them some of the idealism of their youth. They believe that, through hard work and teamwork, they can fix or improve things. Problems can be solved, and solutions can be found. Anything is possible.

Trailing Boomers, however, are a little less optimistic when it comes to finances. The recession hit them during their prime spending years, and as a result, they were left with very little room to build wealth through extra savings. With financial planning, these Boomers tend to operate with a Gen X perspective: skepticism, weariness, and the belief that their financial future is all on them.

3. **Young at heart.** Baby Boomers tend to think of themselves as 10–15 years younger than they really are. Many of them are planning to work beyond traditional retirement age because working helps them feel vibrant, youthful, and engaged. They'll do almost anything to avoid feeling old.

4. **Workaholics.** Boomers brought their competitive spirit and sense of commitment and hard work to their jobs, giving rise to the term "workaholic." Boomers tend to measure productivity in the amount of time spent at work. Moreover, Boomers believe that your work ethic should be visible for everyone to see. If it's not, you're probably not working that hard, in their view.

5. **Proud of success.** Boomers believe the rewards for success should be visible and tangible. This means that they are keen on awards and recognition for accomplishments. They have worked hard, and they feel they deserve the spoils of that hard work. Furthermore, they want the rewards to be visible to everyone.

6. **Team players.** Baby Boomers often like to think of themselves as part of a team. They are champions of teamwork in the workplace and community. They feel that getting along and building relationships is the way to get

things done. They would rather work with those who feel like part of their team.

7. **Into face time.** Baby Boomers generally like to do business face to face. They feel like that's the kind of interaction that really counts. Even though phone calls and emails might be more efficient and are often necessary, they don't offer the personal touch that Boomers deem as critical to maintaining relationships. They view face time as "real" work time and other kinds of interactions as peripheral and supplemental.

8. **Into custom solutions.** The Boomers were the original "me" generation. They often feel like they've earned the right to something special. Boomers are happier if they feel like they are receiving solutions focused uniquely on them.

9. **Nostalgic.** Even though the 1950s and '60s are now more than 40 years past, Baby Boomers have never really let go of them. They tend to remember their youth fondly on every occasion.

10. **Friends with their children.** Boomers frequently preferred to "get to know" their kids and do fun activities with them, almost as peers. As their children mature into young adults, that relationship continues. Both Boomer parents and their still relatively young Millennial children tend to advise and consult each other about big financial decisions. This type of parent-child relationship is the first of its kind.

Seven Financial Traits of Baby Boomers

1. **Short on retirement funds.** The Baby Boomers are approaching retirement in the shadow of the worst economic downturn in generations. According to a recent Willis Towers Watson survey, 77% of Baby Boomers have become more concerned about the security of their retirement benefits over the last two or three years. To add insult to injury, only 30% say that retirement saving is a top priority, and most have unrealistic expectations about the money they will need.

   For example, Boomers expect future nursing home care to cost an average of $46,000, when actual current needs average almost twice that ($90,000). As the leading edge of the Baby Boomer generation entered retirement age, they began to realize that they may not have done all that they should have. Eighty percent (80%) of Boomers wish they had saved more and on a more consistent basis. As result, they are increasingly anxious about their ability to maintain the lifestyles to which they've become accustomed.

Trailing Boomers are in even worse shape as they've used their resources to support their children through expensive educations and beyond (including adult children still living at home). When these individuals entered the workforce, pensions still existed, so these Boomers didn't get an early start on self-funded retirement. They simply haven't been able to get the financial foothold of their Leading Boomer peers.

2. **Postponing retirement.** As a consequence of this savings gap, many are finding that their plans for retirement must be revised. Many are simply postponing it. A full 51% expect to retire after age 65 (and 15% plan to never retire). The ranks of adults over 65 in the workforce began to swell in 2011 as the first Boomers reached the traditional retirement-age milestone. In a related 2016 Gallup survey, the average age of *expected* retirement (among nonretirees) is 66, which is a year higher than it was in 2015.

Many of the Boomers who are retiring early or on time are doing it due to health issues. In other words, they don't want to retire, but their failing health is forcing them to retire.

3. **Still supporting family.** Boomers are using their would-be retirement savings to help out family members from generations who are having an even tougher time. While most Boomers do not have young children, almost 21% have at least one child 18 and older living at home.

    Seventy-four percent (74%) of Millennials receive financial support from their parents, with support ranging from health insurance to utilities, vacations, and rent. Keep in mind that less than half of Millennials are under 21. Boomer parents report an average of $10,000 in annual expenses related to supporting an adult child. A quarter of these Boomers indicate that this ongoing support is a reason for their delayed retirement.

    In addition, many Baby Boomers are helping their Millennial children or grandchildren realize the dream of homeownership. In one survey of Millennials, 65% indicated their parents had contributed to the necessary down payment on a home purchase.

A handful (4%) of Boomers are "sandwiched," caring for their aging parents who may be in their 70s or 80s while also responsible for young children—a consequence of marrying and bearing children much later than was common in past generations. As Baby Boomers advance in age, this phenomena will only increase, especially as Millennial children show a propensity to remain in their parents' pockets until well into their 20s.

4. **Vanishing inheritances.** Boomers are losing their own expected inheritance to their parents' longevity. Their parents' generation has reached their late 70s and has as much as a fifty-fifty chance of living well into their 80s with many living into their 90s. Thanks to medical and longevity gains, 85-and-over is the fastest growing age group in the nation. But thanks to that longevity, the Boomers expected inheritance is shrinking as long-lived retirees use their resources to support themselves. Accordingly, many

Boomers are lowering their expectations for an inheritance.

Likewise, many Baby Boomers, even wealthy ones, have no intention of leaving an inheritance. Instead, they plan to use their fortunes on themselves. In a survey by U.S. Trust, only 53% of wealthy Boomers (compared to 59% and 65%, respectively, of Gen Xers and Millennials) stated that it is important to leave a financial inheritance to children or heirs. In addition, 37% of wealthy Boomers feel that their children need to be at least 35 years-old before they will have the maturity necessary to handle the money they will receive.

This marks a sharp departure from attitudes among previous generations and from traditional financial planning. Many Boomers have simply expressed the desire to enjoy the fruits of their labors and feel that they have already doled out their fair share for kids' tuition, travel, lifestyle, room and board, down payments, etc. It's their turn. If you can't take it with you, they reason, why leave it behind?

5. **Two generations in one—both culturally and financially.** Although Leading and Trailing Boomer subgroups share many of the same formative experiences and attitudes, they are at different life stages and may have different spending priorities. Leading Boomers began to reach the traditional retirement age in 2011. For the most part, their children are adults, and these Boomers are focused on concluding their careers, transitioning to retired life, and securing their children's and their own futures. Many of them are grandparents. Many have moved to new homes (closer to children, requiring less maintenance, or to a dream location), shifted their assets to more conservative investments, generally downsized and simplified their lifestyles, and focused on preserving their health and longevity.

On the other hand, the youngest members of the Trailing Boomers group may still have children in school and are in mid-career. Because the retirement age will likely increase over the next few decades, they may be as many as 25 years away from retirement. They will have different priorities such as getting their kids through school and off to college, improving and upgrading their homes and lifestyles, and building their personal wealth. The distinction between the goals of these Boomer subgroups is especially important for sales professionals in the fields of financial services and retirement planning.

Some observers have also noted a more subtle difference in outlook or mind-set between the older and younger groups of Baby Boomers. For the most part, Leading and Trailing Boomers seem to share the qualities of ambition and competitiveness, and both seem to be enthusiastic consumers. However, Trailing Boomers seem to have a tinge of the skepticism that we usually associate with Generation X.

Leading Boomers have reason to remain a little more idealistic and optimistic than Trailing Boomers. The "system" that they've worked in and paid into has largely been there to repay them. They have taken some financial hits from the Great Recession, but for the most part, their investments have grown with the country's prosperity and will be there to reward them. They still have reason to pursue the dreams they have always looked forward to. Still, as has been discussed, many are not feeling adequately prepared.

Trailing Boomers had less time to accumulate wealth before economic setbacks. They may not have lost as much, but they haven't gained as much, either. They have felt the pain of economic downturns more sharply, and are more similar to Gen Xers in terms of their debt level. They may be less optimistic and more pragmatic. For them, the "dream" has been diminished and postponed. They probably prefer to know the cold, hard facts while trying to find the best-case scenario.

6. **Anxious.** Though the great recession is behind them, many Baby Boomers still feel it in their bones, and the anxiety it caused has been replaced with anxiety about the state of today's economy. The stability of China's economy is constantly in the headlines. The lack of growth in Western economies is in the headlines. Great Britain's vote to leave the EU has,

likewise, caused a great deal of uncertainty, and the impact of it on the financial community is far from clear. While the stock market is up at the time of this writing, there is no consensus that it will remain high or even climbing. The future is very uncertain for Boomers' retirement funds. Theirs is a constant state of anxiety: Stay in the stock market? Pull out and claim the gains? Or some combination? With recent Department of Labor rulings against the financial services industry, you can see why the Baby Boomers feel so much anxiety around their financial situation.

7. **Self-reliant ... or so they tell themselves.** Baby Boomers are confident in themselves and their decisions. They built their kingdoms and can stand proud in being self-sufficient. This is not translating to financial planning, however. Most Boomers are not making the plans that will actually keep them self-reliant. This can be an entry point for advisors. If you can show that working together will help them stay independent, you can appeal to their egos while being viewed as an ally.

Fourteen Ways to Connect with Baby Boomer Clients

1. **Courtship and story time.** Invest in relationships with Boomers. Satisfy their need for face time with lunches, dinners, outings, meetings, or excursions. Make sure they understand that their business is important to you. Send letters or handwritten cards at appropriate times. Call them personally to "check in." And call them to let them know about special promotions and offers.

   Boomers want to know about your background and the background of your firm, so be ready to introduce yourself to them and tell them about yourself. Even if it is your first day on the job, even it is your first day in the workforce, you need to have a story to tell.

   Try this: "I began in this business after a five-year stint in the accounting world with one of the big firms. The transition from there to here was exciting for me because I've always been curious about financial services. Prior to the accounting job,

I attended my state university. My hometown is on the coast, and I still have family there today."

Or: "Our firm began ten years ago. I was part of a larger group, and I didn't feel we were providing the level of service our clients deserved, so I explored starting a small shop with a few other advisors who shared my thoughts. In the last ten years, we've gone from a struggling start-up to having a reputation as the best, most personable team out there. We love our clients, we dote on them, and we feel that is the right thing to do since they're putting a lot of trust in our services."

2. **Personal communication.** Most Boomers prefer face-to-face communication to the electronic version for most big decisions. Therefore, they will likely view a meeting, or at least a person-to-person phone call, as the proper setting for financial and business matters. For Boomers, face time equals work

time. Other kinds of communication are considered supplemental and best reserved for basic data exchange.

Gen Xer and Millennial advisors, in particular, need to take care that Boomer clients receive personal, face-to-face communication on a regular basis. These two generations often consider electronic communication more efficient. While that may be the case, personal communication, including the eye contact offered in person, is what truly matters to most Baby Boomers. Remember, Baby Boomers aren't loyal to email, text messages, or encrypted PDFs. They're loyal to people. Get to know their personal communication preferences and use those forms of communication whenever possible.

Try this: "How do you like to be contacted? Is there a best time of day to call if I need to speak to you? Do you prefer I use your work email, or do you have a personal one you'd prefer? When do you prefer to meet on issues like these?"

3. **Feature trusted names.** Boomers are attracted to the tried and true, the well-established. Brand-name funds or endorsements from well-known publications will go a long way toward establishing legitimacy and confidence in Boomer clients. Tell the story behind the brands and elaborate on their success. For Boomers, the history and the pedigree of the product matter a great deal. Learn as much as you can about a product and be ready to tell that story.

   > *Try this:* "This index fund was started 15 years ago by a titan in the industry. It's been written about in all of the leading financial publications and is perennially at the top of its class. It really is *the* fund in this category."

4. **Selling is OK.** The Boomers are not adverse to sales and advertising. They understand that sales and marketing are essential to successful businesses and see them as perfectly honorable professions. They are accustomed to, and

comfortable with, traditional sales techniques and approaches. Boomers and Matures will give you the opportunity to sell in the way that you've learned to. Find out what their needs and wants are. Put your products' best features forward and don't forget the bells and whistles. Ask for their business.

Again, if you're a Gen X or Millennial advisor, this may be uncomfortable because it is typically not the way you'd prefer to conduct business. However, if bringing more Boomers to your practice is important to you, you must learn to ask for the business. It will get easier, and, frankly, the Boomers respect it.

> *Try this:* "I'm asking you to consider joining us here."
>
> *Or:* "What factors will you use to make your decision? I'd like to address each one with you because I'd be proud to have your business."

5. **Show optimism.** Boomers are largely upbeat and prefer optimistic and upbeat people. Get

your smiles and your optimism tuned up for Boomer meetings. Don't try to be a Pollyanna, but maintaining a cheerful demeanor will make an impression on Boomers. Share some good news about a portfolio or a market. Emphasize the ways in which your offerings generate positive results and experiences. This may be especially tough for Gen X advisors because, as a generation, they boast about their ability to "call it like they see it." However, in dealing with Baby Boomers, you need to learn to be optimistic.

> *Try this:* "This category is really performing. We've made some great choices here, and this direction looks really promising."
>
> *Or:* "The best thing about these bounces in the market is that we're dollar cost averaging, and that means we're buying low during the bounces. In the end, it will play out well for us."

Another caveat regarding Trailing Boomers: they are looking for honesty with their optimism; they expect a dark side, so don't ignore it. Rather, show them how you'll deal with it. If your projections rely on an aggressive strategy, let them know that. They will respect your ability to recognize and confront uncertainty head-on, as long as you have a plan to work with it. Be optimistic in your ability to help them achieve their goals and realistic in the approach to getting there. If reaching their goals will take hard work and tough decisions (and it likely will), tell them at the outset and encourage them to see the potential rewards.

6. **Help them get control.** Boomers are always looking for ways to manage their busy, over-scheduled lives. If your services can make their financial lives more streamlined and less complicated, they will appreciate it. Highlight products, services, or features that "will do the work for you."

   Beware, however, of promoting too much technology—that may make things seem more complicated for some Boomers, not easier. Some Boomers may want the cool app on their smartphone, but don't assume they all do. Too much technology talk runs the risk of driving Boomers away. If they don't understand the technology or fear working it, they often don't object to what you're showing them. Instead they vanish, seeking a simpler, less complicated way of learning about their account.

> ☀ *Try this:* "This is so easy to manage and track—just check these major indexes, and you'll know how you're doing."
>
> *Or:* "Our monthly statements are simple to understand. The front page provides all the information you need to know about how your investments are faring. There's more in-depth content later in the report, but the front page gives you a fine rundown."

7. **Be a team player.** Boomers value teamwork, so conduct yourself as a member of their financial team. You are not an advisor or an agent; you are a team member. And the Baby

Boomer definition of team is pretty simple: if you need me, I'm there. Demonstrate that commitment in your client relationships.

> ·(๓)· **Try this:** "I appreciate your business and the opportunity to be part of your team. Let's tackle this together and see if we can find the best solution."
>
> *Or:* "I don't see myself simply as an advisor or sales person. This isn't about a transaction; I'm your team-mate for your financial goals. Tell me what you want, and I'll do all I can to help you achieve it."

8. **Customize it.** The original "me" generation has a bit of ego to address, so if you are able to offer customization to fit their exact needs, you will have an edge. Do not enter the conversation assuming you already understand their needs. Always ask. Let them know that you can provide a solution that is unique to their needs. Then customize your solution to meet their needs. Subtly emphasize that you recognize their uniqueness. Don't make

a fuss over it; just let them know that you are aware that they are unique.

> 💡 *Try this:* "You've had a great career and done some amazing things. This approach really suits your values and your accomplishments."

9. **Don't make them feel old.** Boomers often think of themselves as at least 10 years younger than they really are. After all, "50 is the new 40 is the new 30…" and so on. Speak and sell to them the way they think of themselves—fit, active, energetic, and current. Avoid terms such as "active adults," "mature," "older adult," "50 plus," and even "middle-aged." Avoid describing something as "right for someone your age" or a product that is "good for where you are now." Boomers will hear that as "right for an old person like you."

   Also, keep in mind that the Baby Boomers, more than any other generation, like to reminisce. They love nostalgia. What this means to you is that you may spend a good bit of time listening to them remember the way things used to be. Get used to it. It's part of developing the Baby Boomer relationship.

> *Try this:* "Since you are looking to do some active travel a great deal over the next few years, you may wish to consider downsizing your home and using the profit to fund your travel plans. I've heard a lot of buzz about the new Arts District. It is supposed to have a very youthful vibe to it."

10. **Visible Rewards.** Boomers are competitive, like to win, and like to be rewarded with visible signs of success. Offer Boomers rewards for doing business with you. Is there a Thank You gift that they can subtly display in their office or home? A nice pen? Paperweight? Golf shirt? Let Boomers know that you recognize their contribution to your business and then give them a way to remember and display that contribution as an achievement.

> *Try this:* "It's important for our company to have accounts like yours.

This is a symbol of how much we value your business."

Or: "I was thinking about our last conversation, came across these logo golf balls in the company catalog, and thought of you."

Or: "It's been 10 years since you opened your account with us. And while this is only a golf shirt, I hope you'll take it as an acknowledgment that we value and appreciate your business."

11. **Find the right level of technology.** Do not assume that Baby Boomers are comfortable with all of the forms of communication you take for granted. Do not assume that they are uncomfortable. Baby Boomers are adopting technology at an accelerating pace. Still, many of them are hesitant—especially when it comes to finances.

Many Boomers have become adept at technology, but most still value the human touch. Even if a Boomer is comfortable with email and other kinds of messaging, you will still want to supplement that with old fashioned notes, letters, cards, and phone calls from time to time, unless your customer specifically prefers that you not. If you have a new "intuitive" client dashboard, ask whether they'd like a demo before telling them how user friendly it is.

> *Try this:* "Many of our clients have accounts with a variety of companies—insurance, investments, loans, you name it. We created a new client portal that lets you bring all of those accounts into one view, so you can always see your whole financial picture. We can set you up and schedule a time to walk through all of the features using your accounts, if you are interested."

12. **The children matter.** Boomer parents usually have their kids in tow—whether physically or emotionally—even if the children are adults. They tend to stay in regular contact,

talking several times a day. The Boomers are influenced by their children's input, and their children will often do product research for them. Be prepared for their children to be influential in some way in the sales process.

> 💡 *Try this:* "I know many of the financial decisions you are making are for the benefit of your children—both near- and long-term—and it can be strange to discuss them with your family. Would you like to schedule a lunch with your children where we can talk about the areas of your plan that will affect their own financial planning? I can put together a summary for you to preview."

Be respectful of the children's presence and input. Utilize some Millennial selling approaches to connect with Boomers' children. You can even preempt the children's research efforts by giving them some online resources as a place to start looking. Do not discount or dismiss the children's opinions. Their Boomer parents certainly won't.

For some Boomers, you will also need to carefully convince them to be pragmatic in the way they manage their finances. Many are still covering expenses for their adult children—a practice which can ultimately harm the parents' ability to achieve their retirement plans. Without dismissing their concern for their children, you may need to encourage them to focus on their own future and allow their kids the satisfaction of handling their own responsibilities.

See page 57 for more on this phenomenon.

13. **Ego rules.** The Boomers are proud of their work ethic and their accomplishments. Let them know that you recognize and appreciate what they have done. Ask about the items and images they have on display. Ask them to tell you their story. Tell them that they deserve to be rewarded. Help them feel victorious.

Interestingly, Boomers are more likely to seek help for car repairs (something most know they cannot do for themselves) than for financial planning (which they think they understand). In fact, more than 50% of Boomers do their own research and make their own financial decisions. As a result, their willingness to seek assistance is something that can be applauded.

Help give them the sense that they are building and working toward something big, and that their decisions to seek help, as well as your shared approach to their financial plan, fit into a vision for a better and brighter future.

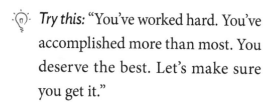 *Try this:* "You've worked hard. You've accomplished more than most. You deserve the best. Let's make sure you get it."

14. **Show your work, ask for the business.** Once you have made a connection with Boomers, established yourself as competent and knowledgeable, and demonstrated that you understand their needs, you can offer them a solution that you have devised to match what they want. Then you can ask to move to the next step. As you move through each step, let them

know what you are doing. Follow through with them, and follow up to let them know that you are still working for them and that you want the sale. Once you show them that you have the ability to deliver what they want, they probably won't shop around elsewhere.

Try this: "We've carefully matched this to your profile and, after some research, and more than a little due diligence, we put together what we think is a perfect package. We'd really like you to consider taking the next step once you've looked over it."

Boomers and Their Children

Your relationship with your Baby Boomer clients should lead to opportunities for you to work with their Millennial children. The common belief is that the Millennials will not do business with their parents' advisors. If you treat the Boomers' children the same way that you treat Boomers, that will be true. Generationally savvy advisors must understand that how they introduce themselves to, talk to, and follow-up with Millennials will be different than how they communicate with their parents.

Getting an introduction is not easy, even when your relationship with a parent is strong. Plant seeds with Baby Boomer parents early on to show that you care about their children's financial success, too. Ask questions like, "What do you foresee for your childrens' financial future now that they are entering adulthood?" And, the straightforward, "Is there anything we can do to help your children with their own financial management as they move into adulthood?"

Let the parents make the introductions and run the show. Prepare an email for your client to forward to his or her children. Make sure this email appeals to both the

Boomer parent—with a brief recap of your business relationship—and then addresses the issues you know to be important to the Millennial child. Ask the parent to forward the email and allow the child to follow up.

Know that when Millennial children receive this email they will probably go online and check you out. Follow the social media tips discussed later in this book to make sure your electronic first impression will hit the mark.

When you reach out to your Boomer clients' Millennial children, introduce yourself quickly, whether in person or over the phone. One of the best ways to start is by saying simply, "So, tell me what I need to know about you." And be quiet. Resist the urge to fill the silence as the other person forms their reply. Listen. Smile and nod. Take notes from time to time. And ask clarifying questions. Let them do the talking. Don't pressure them to open an account or start investing with you. Your job is to simply make them aware of who you are and the services that you offer. In their terms. Using their language. On their own timeline.

Doing it this way, you're much more likely to do business with your clients' children.

SIX KEY ADVISOR QUESTIONS FOR PREPARING TO WORK WITH BOOMERS

Ask yourself:

1. What is my story? Personal stories, yours or theirs, are meaningful to Boomers. Be prepared to tell your story and to ask Boomers for theirs.

2. Am I ready for the Boomer transition into retirement? How do I establish my value or my product or service as the Boomers move into their next stage of their life? How do I transition with them?

3. Are there accounts that represent an opportunity for me to do business with the next generation of clients in the same family?

4. If I am a Baby Boomer (or my firm has several), am I capturing important client information to transfer knowledge when I reach retirement? Is this an organized process or am I "winging it?" This is a high-risk area for many practices; work hard to transfer your strong relationships to the next generation of

advisors, so your clients remain confident in the practice's ability to achieve their goals.

5. If I am a Baby Boomer, do I have a plan for introducing the next generation of internal talent to my clients, so they'll know my firm has considered succession planning and longevity? Include younger advisors in client meetings; explain their role and why they add value to the team. Have regular lunch or coffee meetings where senior advisors share a client story.

6. Is there any part of my office or firm that may cause my Boomer customers to have to ask embarrassing questions due to technology or other things that are assumed to be common knowledge by younger generations? How can I solve this? No one, regardless of his or her generation, likes the feeling of embarrassment.

ADVISING GENERATION X

THE XERS

Numbering around 60 million, Generation X makes up just under 20% of the population. It is a smaller generation than the ones before and after it, but it will be as financially important over the next several decades. Members of Generation X are now in their late thirties to early fifties and are entering their peak earning years. At work, they are often in leadership and senior management roles. In the marketplace, their life stage makes them a leading or key demographic in the market for real estate, automobiles, appliances, electronics, and financial services. They own homes and are raising families, buying cars, and investing in their retirements.

Gen X is also referred to as a sandwich generation, increasingly responsible for the care of adult children (48%) and parents (21%) or even both (15%) as well as themselves. As a result, their finances are pulled in many different directions.

FOUR REASONS GEN X CLIENTS MATTER

1. **They are peaking.** Members of Generation X are entering their peak earning years, typically beginning around 50 years old, well on their way down their career paths. Well-educated and tech-savvy, they have proven themselves diligent careerists and are moving into leadership positions. This generation also has the highest average income of any generation. Yet their average assets are still low and have not increased since 2007.

   Over the next two decades, they should make more money than at any point in their lives. They are also raising families and making big-ticket purchases. Ten percent are in the market for home ownership and roughly 67% are homeowners. They are in the most expensive chapters of their lives.

2. **They are planning.** Members of Generation X are approaching the age when they need to plan for retirement and financial security. For account executives and advisors who work in the field of banking, investments, retirement planning, and retirement services, Generation X will become the most important market as Baby Boomers move into retirement.

   Due to their immense responsibilities, and the previously mentioned expensive chapter in life, Gen Xers may not be planning as far ahead as you would think, or prefer. Their current focus is near-term, so their planning is focused on reducing debt and paying for their children's education. Help them with those goals, so they can look beyond the near-term to a retirement that feels far away but depends on long-term planning.

3. **They are loyal.** Once services, brands, and key individuals get the Gen X seal of approval, members of Generation X will stick with them. Once they've gone through the research and trouble to determine a firm's quality,

authenticity, and value, they are not inclined to go elsewhere. If they find a financial advisor they feel they can trust, it's not worth their time to put another one through such vetting. Again, if you can get through to Gen X, you will likely have a long-term client. That said, they are quick to quit you if you lose that trust. While Gen Xers do not need the intimate attention the Boomers prefer, they should not be taken for granted.

4. **They lead the way online.** While Millennials are usually thought of as the most tech-friendly generation, Generation X approaches or equals them in almost every category. For example, members of Generation X were the first to embrace online banking. This means that Gen Xers will continue to be avid consumers of technology products and services. It also means that as online commerce is further incorporated into almost every business, including financial advisory firms, Gen X will be one of the principal target demographics for that commerce.

Eleven Classic Gen X Client Attitudes and Characteristics

1. **Tough customers.** Ever skeptical and cynical, they tend not to believe any claim or slogan until they see it backed up with cold, hard facts. They've heard countless pitches, jingles, and promises, and don't think there's anything to back them up. This applies to financial advisors, employers, politicians, and everyone else. Members of Generation X are likely to quiz and grill financial professionals like no other generation. They want to know "why" a lot. Why does it cost that much? Why is it only available in that configuration? Why is it packaged that way? Why are you so anxious to sell me this? Don't take it personally or as an attack on your firm's or your credibility. Gen Xers were raised in the information age and are naturally suspicious. They just want straight answers.

2. **Know a phony when they see one.** Because Xers insist on the truth, the whole truth, and nothing but the truth, there's no sense in giving them anything but the straight story.

If they have the sense that someone is less than completely honest with them, they will write that person off for good. Obviously, no scrupulous financial advisor sets out to deliberately deceive people, but the bar is set higher for Gen X. In fact, the recent Department of Labor ruling regarding fiduciary responsibility is more proof to a Gen Xer that, too often, advisors don't have client interests at the forefront. If you don't tell them everything they should know at the outset, they will assume you are hiding something from them. Transparency is key.

3. **Smart and tech-savvy.** Members of Generation X are more educated than any generation before them in terms of the number of degrees and the number of years spent in high school and college (although the Millennials will surpass them). They will often educate themselves about investments and finance. Likewise, they tend to "stalk" firms, products, and services until they find exactly what they are looking for.

They will Google advisors and firms, ask peers for opinions, visit offices (often multiple times), and compare offerings. They will decide what they want and whom they want it from—and you may not have even met them yet. By the time they are ready to act, they will assume they know more than a financial advisor until proven otherwise.

They are the epitome of the self-educated consumer, and that puts them squarely in the driver's seat. Do not ignore this truth.

4. **Their referrals are golden.** Because of their "stalking" behaviors, they seek referrals from their peers, colleagues, and friends and put a lot of trust in those recommendations. They know how thoroughly their friends research their purchases and, because of this, know that their buying decisions have been thoroughly vetted. It is not uncommon for them to share research, organized into a spreadsheet, with friends who are shopping for the same thing. Word of mouth has always been the best sales tool. Gen X has ramped it up.

5. ***Carpe diem.*** After growing up in an era of disappointments and broken promises, Gen Xers have learned not to count on much in the future. They saw their parents and grandparents devote years to careers and companies, only to be laid off or have their pension programs cancelled. Often, the future that was always supposed to be better and better just looked worse and worse. Consequently, they learned that if there's something out there that's good for the taking, do it now. They are perfectly willing to work, but they want to enjoy the rewards sooner rather than later. *Carpe diem*, which means "seize the day," is Gen X's approach to life.

   This approach ties into their finances and financial planning. Generation X is 20% less likely than Boomers to plan and save for the future, even though Boomers had more systems in place to support them into the future. Gen X lives for today, because that is all they believe they can count on.

6. **No deference.** Countless authority figures have let Generation X down. Beginning with

Watergate, the leaders of Generation X's youth have been embroiled in scandal after scandal. In the 1980s, a handful of famous preachers as well as some major churches turned out to be harboring dark secrets. Product failures and recalls cast doubt on the intentions of manufacturers and corporations. The savings and loan collapse made banking seem like a house of cards, and once it had regained credibility, along came a housing bust that led to the Great Recession. As a result, Generation X does not confer positional trust and respect before it is earned. In fact, authority figures, including corporations and financial professionals, must work harder to demonstrate that they deserve more respect than an average stranger.

The trust of Generation X is hard-earned, and it can be lost with a single misstep.

7. **Enough with the Boomers.** Generation X was raised in a Baby Boomer world, and they kind of resent it. Most popular culture in the 1970s and 1980s seemed to be created by, for, and about Baby Boomers. Xers watched

their parents and older siblings go whole hog into fads. First, the Boomers were flower children, then they had disco fever, and then they became urban cowboys. As they aged, they flooded pop culture with Boomer nostalgia. Gen X's resentment of the Boomers comes partly from overexposure and partly from the feeling that, for all of their sound and fury, Boomers actually accomplished very little for future generations—as if they threw a big party and left it to Gen X to tidy up. This hurdle deserves special consideration from Boomer-generation financial advisors.

Part of this tension may also stem from the sense that Boomers are "sticking around" past their expiration date in their careers and professions, blocking the path for Xers to ascend to their career peaks. Boomers' reluctance to retire, whether based in culture, personality, or economics, is the source of some career frustration. Generation X fears being passed over as Boomers stay longer, passing the torch to Millennials rather than the Xers who feel it is their turn at the top.

8. **Parents spending quality time.** Generation X was the first generation raised more as their parents' friends than as subordinates. With fewer children in each family and most parents at work most of the time, parenting began to focus on spending "quality time" with children to compensate for the lack of family togetherness. Kids were allowed to stay up late to watch TV with their parents or to sit at the table and listen while adults talked. This may contribute to the Xers lack of deference to older authorities; they tend to see everyone as peers. Indeed, many still consult with their parents on important financial decisions and vice versa, a trend that becomes more even pronounced with Millennials.

Additionally, Generation X is upping the ante with how they raise their own children. Applying *carpe diem* thinking to their children as well, Xers want their children to have things and experiences that may have once been considered a luxury. Fear of missing out (FOMO) and keeping up with the Joneses—especially when it comes to their children—is an expensive endeavor.

9. **Fend for themselves.** At the same time, culturally and economically, many Xers were left to fend for themselves when growing up. Gone were the days when dad worked all day, mom stayed home and took care of the kids, and everyone joined together for a family meal at the end of the day. Instead, as times got tougher, both mom and dad had to work and left a "latchkey" for Gen X kids to let themselves in when they got home. Day care services became increasingly common as families tried to figure out what to do with the kids while they were busy. In addition to dual careers, most of the Xers' parents also pursued active social lives longer than had been the norm in the past, leaving even less time for their children. Consequently, Xers are accustomed to being left to their own devices and figuring out things for themselves.

10. **Guarded.** Gen Xers are guarded about their personal information and their personal space, and they do not go to a financial advisor to make friends. For Xers, questions like "How are you doing?" and "Are you looking

for something?" are borderline personal inquiries. In fact, a seemingly benign "What are you looking for?" is likely to be met with annoyance as they want to know who you are and what you do, so they can see if that matches their goals. "If I decide you make the cut, then I'll tell you what I'm looking for." This is also why Xers do so much online prep work when evaluating products and services. They want to get past the process and into the work.

They probably won't seem interested in casual chatter, banter about the weather, or sharing their plans for their weekend. Again, don't take it personally. They are there on a mission, and that mission is not to make friends.

11. **Challenging.** Members of Generation X are likely to grill financial professionals like no other generation. They want to know "why" a lot. They demand to be an educated consumer. If they don't understand something they'll simply not buy it. Many Boomers get frustrated, feeling like they're being doubted

or that their years in the business should give them instant credibility. Not to Gen X. Gen Xers were raised in the information age and are naturally suspicious. They just want straight answers.

Seven Financial Traits of Generation X

1. **The biggest losers.** In net worth, that is. Recent Census and Federal Reserve figures created jaw-dropping headlines when they revealed that most Americans' net worth has declined to the point that it is no greater than it was 20 years ago. During that decline, no generation lost more net worth, by percentage, than Generation X. Forty-four percent (44%) experienced retirement plan losses, and a full 68% are still feeling the impact of the market crash. According to the Census Bureau, Generation X households lost close to 40% of their net worth between 2007 and 2010. While their net worth has increased slightly since the end of the recession, in 2013, it was still 26% below what it was in 2007. Because of their life and career stages, Xers have been particularly vulnerable to the effects of the Great Recession and its aftermath. Today, many have yet to regain that footing, and those that have are dubious of the traditional financial channels, which have failed badly. What's to say they won't fail again?

2. **Slow to save.** Despite the cautionary example of Baby Boomers who are barely scraping together enough to retire, Gen Xers are falling behind in retirement savings. A Hewitt Associates report showed that Xers are not setting aside enough for retirement even though 86% say they are concerned that Social Security will not be there for them when they retire. Almost one-third of eligible Gen X and Millennial employees do not participate in an employer-sponsored retirement plan, such as a 401(k) or 403(b). Among Generation X workers who are offered a 401(k) plan or similar, 74% are contributing 10% or less of their salary toward that plan.

3. **Shunning traditional instruments.** Only 30% of Gen Xers have IRAs or Roth IRAs, while nearly 60% participate in a defined employer contribution plan. The sharp drop in interest in IRAs is attributable to economic insecurity. Many stopped contributing to their investments in the past 12 months, citing financial strain. Twenty-seven percent (27%) do not invest at all.

4. **Will need to save more than Boomers.**
Generation X will have to save much more
for retirement than their parents' generations,
according to recent surveys of investment
advisors. The targets will be substantially
higher than they were for Baby Boomers.
Moreover, Congress changed eligibility for
full retirement benefits to age 67 for those
born in 1960 or later. This loss of retirement
income combined with increased life expec-
tancy means that people will need retirement
income for more years, and the typical retirement age is likely to increase over the next
few decades.

A recent GoBankingRates.com survey
estimated that only 27% of Generation Xers
have more than $100,000 in retirement sav-
ings and that almost one-third had no retirement savings. If the general rule of thumb is
that an individual needs 16 times their salary to retire comfortably, that works out to
$1.2 million for a Gen Xer making $75,000.
Getting to those figures is likely to be a tall
order given current contribution rates.

While Gen X hasn't wanted to look far ahead and face this reality, they are beginning to get anxious.

5. **Cautiously warming to saving and investing.** A 2016 survey by the Transamerica Institute found that members of Generation X (along with Millennials) are warming up to the idea of investment. In the survey, 30% of Generation Xers who participate in 401(k) and similar plans have increased their contributions over the past twelve months.

Perhaps because retirement is starting to appear on the horizon, members of Generation X are beginning to feel a sense of urgency in increasing their investment returns. A 2015 survey by MFS Investments found that two-thirds of Generation X investors said that they're "more concerned than ever about being able to retire when they thought they would," which is up from 54 percent in 2014. This has meant, for example, that they are more open to change their investment strategy, in the hope of greater returns. Transamerica found in their 2016 survey that

Generation X is the generation least likely to have their retirement savings mostly in safe havens such as bonds, money market funds, and cash. Most members of Generation X (like Millennials and Boomers) have a relatively equal mix of stocks and safer investments. Interestingly, about 2 in 10 members of Generation X indicated that they don't know what their investment mix is.

6. **Latchkey investors.** When it comes to finance, Gen Xers are most likely to consider do-it-yourself approaches. They are accustomed to looking after themselves, having been the first generation of "latchkey kids" who cared for themselves after school.

   While there are some indications that Generation X is becoming more open to investing, in 2015, about 4 in 10 still reported feeling uncomfortable with investing in the stock market (which is higher than it was in 2013 and 2014). In addition, Transamerica found that almost 7 in 10 admitted they don't know as much about investing as they should. Yet, only 25% of investors indicate that they rely on a financial advisor for investment advice.

In another case of perception vs. reality, 52% of Gen Xers working with a financial advisor have at least $100,000 saved for retirement, while only 27% of those going solo have that much saved.

7. **Midcareer doldrums.** As Generation X nears the career stage when assuming leadership positions at work would be natural, they find themselves stuck between an immovable object and an unstoppable force: the Baby Boomers and the Millennials. Boomers, whether because of need or preference, are signaling that they won't be going anywhere anytime soon. Meanwhile, Millennials are on the march and looking for the fast track up the corporate ladder.

In addition to Boomers not retiring and well-educated, tech-savvy Millennials entering the work force in droves, Xers have to overcome a few other hurdles. For one, they may face resentments from older colleagues as they move into supervisory roles over them.

Additionally, Generation X is not known for its loyalty to employers. By the same token, Xers don't have a great deal of trust in their employers. These perception problems have to be overcome for Xers to advance.

Fifteen Ways to Connect With Gen X Clients

1. **Keep networking short and simple.** Introduce yourself quickly and without fanfare while letting Gen Xers know that you are available if they need something. Instead of a long verbal introduction, you might simply hand them a business card and keep your comments brief. Avoid making them feel pressured. Keep your comments focused on how you help your clients create predictability and safety, and help them meet their future financial goals. Don't focus on your personal background by explaining where you grew up or how long you've been in the profession.

   > 💡 *Try this:* "I'd be happy to tell you about what we offer if you're ever interested. We pride ourselves on being straightforward in what we do. We create and implement financial plans that get our clients where they want to go."

2. **Stay on message.** Typical Gen Xers have little tolerance for idle chatter from salespeople—at

least at the outset of a business relationship. When discussing products and services with Gen Xers, avoid unnecessary verbiage or fuss. They tend to be skeptical of too much hype or promotion. You need to sell the steak; they are not interested in the sizzle, at all. They are interested in the facts: the numbers, the dimensions, the performance, etc.

View your encounter as an information exchange, not a sales call. Xers crave knowledge. They will likely find out everything they want to know about you on their own. Instead of fighting that fact, embrace it. Be prepared to answer "why?" and to refer them to additional, unbiased resources, including side-by-side analyses.

Try this: "I can make a copy of all the documentation if you want to take it home and look it over."

Or: "You can check out all the specs on this website."

Or: "Please do all the research you need; here is a list of what we think are the best sites to check everything out. If anything conflicts with what we've discussed, please let me know what you've found because it is something we need to know about."

3. **Transparency matters.** Let them know right off the bat what is available. If they suspect you are being cagey or if the story changes during the advising process, they will smell a rat. Remember, they are mostly meeting with you to gather information: What is available? How much does it cost? How does it compare to others? Show them where they can go on the web to read up at their convenience.

   If you help facilitate this process, a typical Xer will look favorably on you. But if they feel like you are trying to manipulate the information, they will assume you are deceptive, and they will find someone else. In your efforts to be transparent, you will win more points by being self-deprecating than by knocking others. If you talk poorly about a competitor, Xers will assume you may also talk poorly about them.

-☼- *Try this:* "I'll level with you: I don't think we are currently doing our best in managing those funds and would recommend we look at another option."

Or: "These instruments aren't flashy, but they just keep heading in the right direction. Here, take a look at these graphs."

4. **Authenticity counts.** Gen Xers can spot a phony a mile away. You need to be who you say you are and be able to back up the way you present yourself. If you don't share their style, interests, or tastes, don't pretend you do. When they talk with salespeople, Gen Xers are often probing for clues as to whether or not the person can be trusted.

Avoiding all pretenses and just being who you are is best. If they get a whiff of any phoniness, Gen Xers may simply write you off and move on. If you say you are an expert, be prepared to prove it.

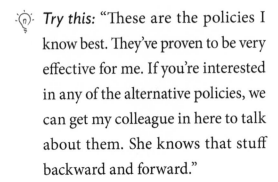 *Try this:* "These are the policies I know best. They've proven to be very effective for me. If you're interested in any of the alternative policies, we can get my colleague in here to talk about them. She knows that stuff backward and forward."

5. **Peers carry weight.** Peer-to-peer testimonials—about yourself as well as your offerings and services—will go a long way toward convincing members of Generation X that you are the person they want to do business with. When you have a good connection with a Gen X client, ask if he or she would be willing to serve as a reference if needed.

Try this: "If I were you, I would want a referral for a business relationship like this one. I have a similar client, and I can arrange for you to ask her some questions about me and how I work with my clients. She's offered to chat with you if you'd like."

Or: "You seem to be well connected in your community, and I suspect that people come to you from time to time for referrals or advice. I'd consider it a privilege to get any referrals from you. You can count on me treating them very well."

6. **Short-term goals.** That is the Gen X approach to life. They tend to have shorter time horizons than other generations. Explain how you can improve their lives today, as well as a few miles down the road.

   Gen X seeks short-term solutions and achievable goals; they don't want to wait for results. In your advising, look to the short- and medium-term horizon, as well as the long-term you are traditionally working toward.

   Try this: "By the end of this year, we should be at this point. We can also allocate some resources here. It's a little riskier, but you could see some substantial gains faster in that category."

Or: "By the end of today's meeting, let's come to some decisions on how to proceed with your allocations. Let's set that as a simple goal for our time together, so we can make sure we're moving in the right direction."

7. **Be online.** Gen Xers aren't as addicted to technology as Millennials, but they are among the leading users of online financial services. Your firm should have an online presence, preferably one that facilitates product research, shopping, and buying. Xers will be frustrated if they can't read about and interact with your company on their own whenever they want, and the way they prefer to do that is on the Web or through smartphone apps. Offer insights free and at their convenience— through articles, blogs and newsletters that help them understand who you are, how you view the current economic climate, and the type of advice you tend to give people in situations similar to theirs.

    Gen Xers will develop a picture of you based on your online activity and personality.

Make sure that is the picture you want, and that it is more than simply your academic and professional resume. Show them who you are:

> For example, in your bio: "While I love my work, my passion outside of work is cooking exotic meals. Often, I scour my city to find the needed ingredients or order them from Amazon, anxiously awaiting their arrival, so I can give a new recipe a try. Most of the time, my family is eager to test out my cooking, but more than once, I've actually seen my wife turn green when eating some of my dishes. She says nothing and quietly dismisses herself from the table."

If there isn't enough information on your site for them to learn what they want to know about you, they may go someplace else where they can find more in-depth information.

8. **Time > Money.** Many Gen Xers value their time more than money. Potential Generation X clients probably won't want to be courted. They are more interested in their time than

in business relationships. To become their advisor, prove your ability to do things right and quickly, not by spending an afternoon on the golf course with them.

If there's a quick and easy source for your information online, let them know about it.

Try this: "I know you're busy. Let me show you how well we can perform for you. What interests you about what we offer? Let me come back and show how you'd benefit from our services. It will be quick and to the point. If you like it, we can talk about next steps."

9. **Options.** When you offer Xers a single solution, they may suspect that 1) you offer this to everyone you meet regardless of their needs or 2) there is an internal promotion, and you'll sell this regardless of whether they really need it or not. Therefore, you need to offer options. Make sure they have the full range of alternatives available to them.

To Baby Boomers an "expert" is someone who has been in the business for years and has the scars to prove it. To Boomers, experts have earned the right to make specific, narrow recommendations to clients. To Gen X, though, this type of rifled focus on a single solution creates unease. "Is this what I need?" they ask, "Or is this what they want to sell me?" The Boomer advisor must learn that their years of history in the business don't matter to the Gen X client. The Gen X client defines an "expert" as the person who will help them become an educated consumer; they tend to define an expert as a teacher.

> Saying something like: "Here are three solutions for you based on our discussions of your needs. Any one of these will work, and I'll explain why and the difference in each one, but here is the entire list for your review. If there is something on this list that interests you, let me know, and we'll go over it."

10. **Back-up plans.** Address their innate cynicism with back-up plans for the inevitable time when a problem arises. Xers often expect problems, and they will appreciate your

willingness to concede imperfection. They will overthink it: What will happen if Plan A doesn't work? Don't take it personally.

Back-up plans are more important to Gen Xers than others. They expect things to fail and plans to fall through. Present proposals that have a Plan B ready if needed. There's no need to go into detail; just let them know you have it.

> ⋅ᖛ⋅ *Try this:* "Based on your needs, I've identified some things that I think will serve you well. If these aren't appropriate for any reason then I have additional ideas, but let's start with these because I think they'll work."

11. **Hand them the reins.** Clients from Generation X often want an unusual amount of involvement in the planning process. They will want to know every detail. They will look over your shoulder while you are entering their data. They will want to know about your procedures and policies, even how much commission you will make. They will try to read the paperwork before they sign. They will see any step that

they don't personally oversee as an opportunity for someone to take advantage of them. Involve them as much as you can in the process. Let them see the nitty-gritty details.

When you are limited by company policy in what you can offer, let them know about the policies and why they are in place. If they can manage and monitor the process online, show them how. Gen Xers want to feel like the process is under their control. Let them.

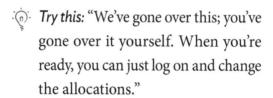 *Try this:* "We've gone over this; you've gone over it yourself. When you're ready, you can just log on and change the allocations."

12. **Appropriate communication.** Members of Generation X typically don't need or want a lot of face or phone time in their business relationships. They do want you to be responsive. They are adept users of mobile technology and pioneered the virtual office. While they value personal time, they don't fully believe in the traditional 9–5 environment. If a question comes to mind during their kid's game on Saturday afternoon, they'll send an

email asking it. Respond, even if you are not working that weekend.

They are not as insistent as Millennials on using only the latest forms of communication, but on the whole, they do prefer them. Ask them how they prefer to be contacted and oblige them. If your business has online investing and allocation options, direct your Gen X customers to them.

> *Try this:* "That's a great question. My initial thought is _____, but I'd like to research further before providing a solid recommendation. You'll hear from me by COB Monday."

13. **Shed some light.** Xers often want to do extensive research and comparisons, so they can feel they have educated themselves sufficiently. They demand to be educated consumers. If you can offer them some background, advice, or information that they were not aware of, it will earn you some respect and esteem in their eyes.

    If you can, share with them what you know—your "inside" information and your firm's data—they will feel like you have let them in on some special intelligence, and their quest to be the most informed investor will be fulfilled.

> *Try this:* "Look, here's all the background material they gave us on this fund. You might find some of this informative."

14. **Don't be aggressive.** After you have provided all the information you have and answered all their questions, leave the ball in the Xer's court. They need space to make a decision. If they feel you have been honest and efficient, and that what you are offering is fair and transparent, most of the time, they will make that decision. Once you have gained respect as an honest and valuable resource, Xers will remain fiercely loyal. Don't try to make the hard close, which risks making them feel like you're selling them something.

> *Try this:* "You'll want to make your own decision on your own time. Whenever you're ready to pull the

trigger, I'm right here. Can I follow up with you next Wednesday around lunchtime to get your feedback and answer your questions?"

15. **Stay true.** Make sure your continuing service matches the initial advising experience. Remember that nearly three-quarters of consumers from the younger generations will switch to a competitor after just *one* bad customer service experience. And 85% of those will tell their peers about it.

Gen Xers will not tolerate poor service after being promised something else. They'll call "bait and switch" on you. Your chances for repeat business and referrals from Generation X depend as much on your follow through as the initial account formation.

Try this: Schedule a recurring quarterly meeting and put it in both of your calendars with a reminder a week out. Let your Gen X client know that you'll certainly bring up important ideas in between, but you want to be sure they make their financial future a priority. Also, let them know that they can reschedule if the timing doesn't work when each meeting comes around.

The Married Gen X Mother

At the top of the list of the most influential consumer and influencer in today's marketplace is the Generation X mother. She's dominating in the marketplace, and she is not afraid to tell all her friends who they should do business with and, more importantly, who they should not do business with.

Today, Generation X women have more education than Generation X men and are slowly catching up in pay. She's highly engaged in her community. She's a discerning buyer. When these factors come together, a Generation X woman becomes the apex consumer in our marketplace.

Historically, financial decision-making has been done by the male head of household, and that certainly remains the case for many households today. But the gen-savvy advisor needs to be aware of the growing influence of the female head of household. She may not simply participate in the meeting. She may, in fact, drive the meeting, asking pertinent questions throughout. Whether she is outspoken or reserved when you meet, she will have a lot to say about how the business proceeds with you. The Generation X female head of household, due to her unique consumer characteristics, has more influence than ever before. Once she becomes a mother, her influence grows greatly—not only with her spouse but also with her peers. She influences her in-laws, her parents, her siblings, and her network. It is a new phenomenon, but it is real.

Treat the Gen X mother—or any head of household—well. Seek her input into decisions. Encourage her to get involved. Don't assume her silence or seeming lack of interest is an indication of indifference. And never, ever ask her if she needs to check with her spouse. In fact, when she's not present, encourage the spouse to discuss important, upcoming decisions with her. She'll learn that you value her input and want to make her a part of the decision.

Treat her well, and she'll tell her friends how good you are to her. Treat her poorly, and her friends will know that, too. Expect the Millennial married mother to take this influence to new levels. Their expectations, combined with their numbers, will make them a force to be reckoned with. Get comfortable with the Gen X mother now, and you'll be ready when the tide hits.

Seven Key Advisor Questions for Preparing to Work with Generation X

Ask Yourself:

1. Many Xers today are in management and leadership positions, ascending their career ladder. Am I noticing this transition in my prospects? My current clients? Am I using their career success to build my business through new networking opportunities or new product sales?

2. Am I prepared to do more of my advising over the phone or through email? Can I make connections and build relationships with less frequent face-to-face interaction? (You may want to start practicing.)

3. Many organizations have a history of releasing only the information needed to the client. The Xers who can't find the information they need get turned off. Is there information that I've traditionally held back that I might now consider making available to my clients?

4. Am I prepared for clients who "stalk" their investments, doing lengthy and deep research to the point that they actually *do* know almost as much as I do about certain investments? Will I feel threatened by that? Or will I compliment them on their research and knowledge, and engage them in sophisticated conversation about what they know and what they think?

5. How do I react to the client who has Googled "retirement plan" or read some articles online and now thinks they're an expert and just wants me to take an order for them? (In some cases, you may wish to have a list of online resources you can direct them to rather than trying to convince them otherwise. In other cases, you may be able to refer to a client story that demonstrates the added value of working with a professional.)

6. Do I have a strategy to compete against robo-advisors? Do I even want to? Be prepared for Gen X prospects and clients to bluntly ask, "Is there a reason I can't just do this using

Personal Capital or Betterment?" Do I want to convince them otherwise or offer to be a resource if the DIY approach doesn't pan out? (There is no right answer, but you should have a strategy you feel confident in.)

7. What does my online first impression say about me? Is it something that an Xer would look at and determine I'd be a fun person to work with and get to know? Or is it a traditional headshot and resume? (As of this writing, LinkedIn is the go-to professional networking site where they'll find you and check you out. Make sure your photo is both recent and interesting. And that you list some nonprofessional and interesting tidbits about you that will make you someone they'd like to meet.)

CHAPTER 5

Advising Millennials

The Millennials

Millennials were born between 1980 and 2000 into a world ubiquitous with technology. As of the most recent census figures, Millennials have become the largest generation in the United States at over 92 million strong. For the majority of their lives, they knew only economic growth. The Great Recession of 2008–2009 was the first time they experienced a major change in the country's economic pace that impacted them personally. They are mostly the children of the Baby Boomers and the oldest Gen Xers, and they have grown up protected, praised, and programmed by their parents.

Millennials don't have as much accumulated wealth as Baby Boomers or Matures, or as much earning power as Generation X—yet. They have yet to reach their earning prime, and many still rely on their parents for financial support. Some Millennials have been in the workplace for quite a few years, and there are quite a few others that are just now launching careers. However, they will be very important clients over the next few decades as they progress in their careers and inherit their parents' assets. They are the future.

For all their promise and potential, Millennials can seem a confounding and frustrating bunch to older generations trying to do business with them, especially if your success depends on understanding and relating to them. Regardless, Millennials are already a hugely important demographic. Their share of net household wealth will quadruple over the next 15 years.

Millennials are also poised to receive significant inheritances in the coming years. Beginning with approximately $140 billion of wealth transfer in 2015, they are estimated to receive $344 billion in 2040. Establishing relationships in advance of this wealth transfer will be critical.

FIVE REASONS MILLENNIAL CLIENTS MATTER

1. **They are the future.** Millennials are projected to control more than $11 trillion in financial assets by 2030. By the end of the next decade, they will be the primary consumers of financial advising and investment services. They already wield tremendous influence over their parents' financial decisions. Cultivating Millennials now offers the potential for creating long-term brand loyalty among clients who will be active in saving, planning, and investing for decades to come.

2. **Size**. Perhaps the most important feature of the Millennial generation is its *size*. It is now the largest generation in American history. Just as Baby Boomers transformed every market in which they participated, the Millennials are already creating and driving new markets, such as those in personal communication, networking, and technology. Their impact on financial services will be no different.

Furthermore, they will be the bulk of advisory clients for years to come. Millennials are poised to dominate the marketplace, just as the Boomers did in their youth.

The way you do business with Millennials will become the way you do business.

3. **Financial power.** Millennials are also important because of their considerable financial power, present and future. Millennials wield between $1 trillion and $1.5 trillion in annual spending power. When spending on housing is removed from the equation, they have already surpassed Generation X in annual spending. This is especially impressive when you consider that some Millennials are still teenagers, and many are in college or in their lowest earning years.

4. **Technology.** Millennials dominate the technology marketplace. This generation is shaping the way we do business online, in terms of both hardware and software. Through their pioneering use of photo-sharing sites like Instagram, online retailers like Amazon

and iTunes, and social networking and media sites like Facebook, YouTube, and Snapchat, Millennials have become the primary architects of the connected marketplace.

They have, in effect, created new real estate for all industries, including financial professionals. For Millennials, these new electronic storefronts and billboards have become every bit as important as traditional brick-and-mortar offices. And the norm for transactions in this new "virtual" office space—fast, easy, connected, and inexpensive—has become the expected standard for any firm, including advisories.

5. **Social currency.** Millennials are the custodians and guardians of social currency today. They can relay social currency to one another with the touch of a button, and are the natural trendsetters because of their age and the size of their generation. Millennials will decide which industries and firms are "with it" and relevant, and the marketplace at large will follow. In order to be seen as current and relevant, firms and industries

will need to understand and manage social currency.

Social currency is gained by linking your products and services with qualities, ideas, and images that generate positive feelings among target consumers and encourage them to advocate for your business in their social environments. It can be measured with metrics such as the number of Twitter followers, Facebook fans, or YouTube hits . Some common generators of social currency are environmental or "green" practices, an emphasis on technology, the use of sleek, minimalist design, quirky individuality, affordability, and simplicity, among others.

FIFTEEN CLASSIC MILLENNIAL CLIENT ATTITUDES AND CHARACTERISTICS

1. **Educated.** Millennials are the most educated generation in America. They graduate from high school and attend college at rates that surpass all previous generations. Female Millennials, in fact, will be the best educated generation in U.S. history, with nearly 40% of 25 to 35 year old women holding a bachelor's

degree or higher in 2015. By comparison, 30% of Boomer women and 20% of Mature women hold similar credentials.

This means that your Millennial clients will consider themselves smart and savvy consumers, able to research instruments and products independent of financial advice. They will appreciate access to resources for detailed research and comparison.

2. **They embrace "Adultolescence."** Millennials have delayed marriage, childbearing, and the traditional markers of adulthood until later ages than any previous generation. In 2015, Millennials' ages ranged from 15 to 35. Only 45% of older Millennials (25–35) are married, which is less than Gen X or Boomers at the same ages. They may still live at home, on their own, or with roommates. Historically, young adults had been their own decision makers and now, with the advent of adultolescence, Millennials are more likely to have more and more multigenerational influencers around them. And they can influence these individuals as well.

3. **Technophiles.** When asked in a survey what makes their generation unique, a quarter of Millennials listed "technology." That's much higher than any other generation rated *any* identifying feature. They value their smartphones and their tablets. They spend more of their money on cell phones than others, they are the leading users of social media and social networks, and they are the most likely group to engage in a wide range of online activities. Most have never known a world without technologies that seem remarkable to older generations. Technology is a given for them, they are dependent on it, and they can be impatient in any setting, or even with any person, that is not technologically up-to-date.

   They look for a wireless (Wi-Fi) network connection wherever they are because they typically have a device that needs to be connected. Even when physically with their peers, they will have a smartphone or tablet and a desire to be online. They will hang around in places where they can connect.

4. **Diverse.** One important characteristic of Millennials is that they are one of the most diverse generations, by race and ethnicity, in American history (iGen, the generation following Millennials, is even more so). Racial and ethnic minorities make up almost 40% of the Millennial generation, compared to 20% of the Matures and 27% of the Boomers. As a whole, Millennials have grown up with an awareness of the diversity of their peers and have been taught to value tolerance and diversity. They hold tolerance as a moral value—more so than other generations—and expect that others will, too. Your Millennial clients are more likely to come from ethnic minorities and likely to find the values of tolerance and diversity appealing. Likewise, they are more likely to disassociate with you, or even call you out, as a result of perceived intolerances or a lack of diversity.

5. **Issue-oriented.** Millennials, more than any other generation, will buy or invest for a cause. They profess more concern about issues

such as environmental and social responsibility than other generations. They remain optimistic about the ability of government and activism to change the world for the better. This means that Millennial consumers will be interested in firms that take a stand or contribute to a cause. Conversely, they will have a dim view of businesses that appear callous or reckless toward their community or the environment, and will turn away from firms that appear to be only in it for the money.

6. **Peer- and group-oriented.** Peer-to-peer recommendations and word of mouth are always important in connecting, but especially so for Millennials. They rank peers as their number one source of information in many important product categories. In fact, according to PricewaterhouseCoopers, Millennials are twice as likely (31%) to turn to friends and family for financial advice as they are to seek advice from a broker or financial advisor (15%). This may be due to their age and the belief that they do not yet

need such services, but it is also consistent with their generational attitudes. Millennials are responsible for much of the viral attention in today's online community—both positive and negative. They are drawn to companies and brands that seem popular among their peers. The right (or wrong) attention at the right (or wrong) time can have tremendous impact on a company, while being virtually impossible to plan or control.

7. **Individualistic.** Although Millennials like to move in groups, are very responsive to their peers, and may fit their generational norms to a "T," Millennials feel strongly that they are unique individuals. This may stem from growing up in a world where each person is treated as special and valuable. Whatever the root, Millennials like to proclaim their individuality through their choices in fashion, music, tattoos, piercings, and customizable accessories. They value their identity. Although they want what their peers have, they want it with a personal twist, something that makes it their own. Thus, Millennial

clients will be drawn to offerings that can be customized or tailored to recognize their individuality. They don't want you to think they are predictable.

8. **Impatient.** Millennials seem accustomed to instant gratification. This may stem from the very attentive parenting that many of them received as children. It may also be the result of growing up in a world of fast food, overnight shipping, and instant downloads. Whatever they want, they usually want (and can often get) immediately. They value their time. They are reluctant to invest a great deal of time in anything unless it is plainly of value to them. Even then, the window of time may be short. If a transaction is complicated or takes longer than expected, Millennials may not stick around. Conversely, transactions that can happen quickly and simply will appeal to them.

9. **Historically optimistic.** For most of their lives, things have gone pretty well. For the most part, when they were growing up, the

economy grew, technology became cheaper, smaller, and more powerful, and just about everyone told them that everything they did was super. They believed it. They are generally inclined to think things are going to work out in their favor. As a result, even during the recession, many Millennials declined entry-level work because they believed something better was right down the road. The post-recession economic climate tested this attitude.

10. **Big goals but no plans.** Millennials have always been told they could be or do anything they set their mind to. As a result, they can be very ambitious with their aspirations; they often shoot for the moon. On the other hand, they may not have enough life experience to know what it takes to shoot for the moon. In extreme cases, they may not realize that just because their parents told them they could be an astronaut, that doesn't mean they will be allowed to bypass NASA training and shoot straight for the moon. Many Millennials may envision themselves as being wealthy

in their future, but they have no idea how they'll accumulate that wealth. They often can't connect the dots from here to there, and they'll need you to educate them on these things. But don't tell them they can't do it—whatever it is. They aren't interested in being told "no." Instead, tell them what it will take; let them decide if they should make a goal adjustment.

11. **Busy and stressed.** Everyone and everything is competing for Millennials' attention. A typical Millennial has more than 500 "friends" on social networks. Many of them send 100 text messages a day. They have spent their lives on busy schedules—bouncing from school to soccer practice to online video games to saving the world. They want and expect customer experiences to be instant and easy.

Millennials tend to steer clear of experiences that are inflexible, intrusive, and that take up time. A very simplistic example is their television watching. Millennials grew up with DVD, DVR, and now, online streaming. They watch the shows they like, when they want to watch them, rather than on the network's schedule. Likewise, the use of cell phone *voice* minutes is *declining* among Millennials. Phone calls are too time consuming and intrusive. They vastly prefer texting, which they also can do at their own convenience.

12. **Parents' friends.** Millennials were raised more as their parents' friends than as subordinate children. As children, their parents made it a point to spend "quality time" with them. As young adults, they are likely to be consulted by their parents for advice. They tend to treat people from all generations as equals, even older generations. They are not disrespectful, but neither are they deferential. They are not accustomed to being spoken down to. When making big financial decisions, many Millennials will consult their parents, or even bring them along. Along the same lines, Millennials are quite likely to influence older generations in their family in important financial choices.

13. **Well-cared-for and programmed.** Through their lives, most Millennials have been carefully cared for, scheduled, and programmed. They are used to parents and adults in their lives working out all the difficult details for them. If they have moved past one item on the agenda, they are ready for someone to announce what the next step is. They will expect their advisory experiences to be orderly and tidy and without loose ends. They will accept guidance that gets them where they want to go.

14. **Texters.** Millennials exchange dozens to hundreds of text messages per day, so they are likely to be looking down and typing with their fingertips in the midst of whatever else they are doing. Millennials will not interrupt their texting for you. They are having multiple ongoing conversations via text message all day long. They prefer texting because it allows them to do other things while they communicate—and they will. Don't be insulted. They often communicate informally, both verbally and in writing, even with people

they do not know. They frequently use texting language or code, omitting formalities and words they deem unnecessary like articles or determiners. When they text you, they expect a response in short order.

15. **Something for nothing.** Millennials, more than most generations, are attracted to offerings that are free or near free. When Millennials were teens, they got in the habit of downloading whatever music and movies they wanted from the Internet for free. When they finally adapted to paying for music, it was to pay ninety-nine cents for a song on iTunes. Their first credit cards came with a free T-shirt, and as kids, they ate free or got a cheap toy. Whereas Gen Xers will look for the catch, Millennials tend to look for the bonus.

MILLENNIAL CAVEAT

The Millennial generation is in a significant transition within their generation right now. Even more than the Boomers who are divided between Leading Boomers already in retirement and Trailing Boomers still in the workforce, the Millennial generation is straddling two major life stages. They are divided between traditional adulthood and "adultolescence." The youngest portion of the Millennials is still in their teens and living that relatively carefree life, while the oldest members of the Millennials are now into their careers for ten years or more and often married with children and a mortgage.

This creates a significant dichotomy within the generation. Research clearly indicates that with the responsibilities of mortgages, child rearing, and marriage, each generation begins to behave more similarly to the generations that came before them. It is important to understand that while behaviors become more consistent with "people in this stage of life" the underlying beliefs of each generation remain. So Millennials may begin to look more like Boomers and Gen Xers in their action; however their beliefs about saving, money, and the financial services industry will remain largely as described here. In other words, who they are is separate from what they do. A savvy advisor will keep generational norms in mind, even when Millennial clients are passing through typical life stages.

Eight Financial Traits of Millennials

1. **They have a long row to hoe.** More than 50% of Millennials would like to retire by age 60 according to a 2015 Fidelity Investments survey, although other research shows that current college graduates should expect to retire at age 75. Millennials will need a retirement savings rate of nearly 20% annually to achieve their aggressive goals, yet they average 7.5%.

   Advisors should counsel younger generations to start planning as soon as possible, to take advantage of employer assistance, and to utilize instruments like Roth IRAs and 401(k) plans, and to delay claiming Social Security. In short, Millennials will have to save much more for much longer than their parents to realize a comfortable retirement.

2. **The Great Recession generation.** Formative experiences occur in a generation's youth, and often come in the form of drastic economic and cultural upheavals. At the height of the recession, only 20% of Millennials reported themselves "very satisfied" with

their economic condition, and only one-third would describe their finances as good or better. In 2015, they are in much better spirits, with 65% describing their finances as doing okay or living comfortably. The feeling of fragility has left its mark, with twice as many Millennials ranking *job security* ahead of a *high-paying job* (40% vs. 19%) in a Pew Research study.

That said, far fewer Millennials (3%) than any other generation indicated that they will never recover from the Great Recession (8% for Generation X and 12% for Boomers). In fact, roughly one in four said that the Great Recession did not impact them at all. They do, however, feel that they will have more financial challenges than their parents— just over 80% agreed that their *generation will have a much harder time in achieving financial security* than their parents' generation. (Of course, Generation X and Baby Boomers responded in the same way when they were asked to compare themselves to their parents!) But Millennials seem to be more optimistic about their financial future than other generations, with 60% indicating that they are confident in being able to retire with a lifestyle they consider comfortable.

3. **Downsizing Their Dreams.** Millennials, already prone to delay milestones like careers and marriage, are putting them off even further as pessimism about their economic outlook and questions about the stability of the economy cause them to downsize their expectations. For the first time in three decades, Gallup shows that fewer than half of Americans believe the next generation will have a better life. In a 2013 research paper on the future of employment, Oxford professors Carl Frey and Michael Osborne estimated that 47% of current jobs are at high risk of being automated over the next 20 years.

The Great Recession has affected Millennials in many ways. Many saw their parents lose jobs and savings, or themselves had difficulty finding employment when entering the traditional workforce. Many are reconsidering educational plans, since advanced degrees no longer lead directly to jobs. Others are planning to avoid traditional investments, like stocks, that let their parents down. And some are simply resigning themselves to a life with less.

A correlating characteristic of this generation is their interest in the "shared" economy. Sharing cars, for example, but not owning one themselves. Or sharing living spaces in favor of buying a home. It's difficult to tell if this is a long-term trend for this generation, a new trend for this age/life stage, or a fad, but it has caught the attention of every industry from automobiles to property and casualty insurance to mortgage companies.

4. **Risk Averse.** Various studies report that Millennials hold a higher percentage of their financial portfolios in cash compared to older generations. This is counterintuitive as this is the generation with the longest horizon (at least for retirement) and, therefore, the most aligned to a more risky growth strategy. But when you recall the Millennial mind-set, this makes sense, even as it makes things difficult for advisors.

Your firm may want to consider adjusting your offerings or recommended strategies to accommodate Millennials' risk aversion by reducing stock exposure, offering higher interest savings accounts, and adding additional features to conservative investment packages.

However, conservative approaches to investment typically don't make much sense for those in their 20s and 30s. Those are the age groups most able to endure risk in the short-term and most likely to reap the long-term benefits that riskier investments can offer. Advisors are hoping that the Millennials' typical optimism about their financial future will reemerge along with their appetite for financial instruments with higher risk and reward. However, if the Recession leaves the same kind of impression on Millennials that other severe downturns left on previous generations, that confidence may be slow to return.

Advisors must develop a "script" designed to create a small appetite for risk in the Millennial generation. No normal income-earning person can save enough to retire; they must invest their savings. Advisors need to develop a story or a parable to make this clear to Millennial clients. Or, at the very least, make sure that Millennial clients are aware that by not accepting some sort of risk in their investments they are willingly making their retirement plan much harder for themselves.

5. **Reluctant to Save.** Despite the cautionary example of Baby Boomers who are barely scraping together enough to retire, Millennials are falling behind in retirement savings. A 2016 Retirement Confidence Study by the Employee Benefit Research Institute showed only 55% of Millennials ages 24–35 had any form of retirement savings (compared to more than 70% for all older age groups). Further, Millennials are less likely than any other generation to contribute to a retirement savings plan not through an employer (such as an IRA or Keogh). Only 21.5% contribute to such a plan.

Interestingly, while 65% of Millennials consider themselves to be "savers more than spenders," according to a 2014 Ameriprise study, 60% of older Millennials had less than $10,000 in savings and investments. Furthermore, of Millennials with access to an employer-sponsored retirement plan, 43% do not contribute enough to get the maximum employer match, and 69% have reduced or are considering reducing their contribution levels.

This attitude makes sense when you consider the financial pressures created by student debt (much higher with Millennials than previous generations) and the salaries commiserate with the early stages of one's career, but they are in absolute opposition to best practices for individuals with a long investment horizon.

One thing on the horizon in many workplaces is an opt-out 401(k) plan where a small portion of employees' salary is put into a 401(k) by default. The employee must request that this NOT happen rather than signing up for it. This has the potential to help Millennials gather some retirement funds early in their careers, but the program is still so new that the long-term results and the opt-out rates are unclear.

6. **Avoiding stocks.** As the leading edge of the Millennial generation dips its toes into investing, they are more leery of the stock market than previous generations. A survey conducted by MFS Investments finds that Millennials are just as likely to keep their investment dollars in cash instruments, like savings accounts and money market funds, as they are to invest in stocks—a more conservative approach than older generations and a more cautious allocation than is normally recommended for young investors.

Millennial fears about the stock market stem from the recession as the scars from those memories run deep. The market is up as of this writing, surpassing previous highs, but to the Millennials, it doesn't feel that way. Many still feel "underemployed" and living paycheck to paycheck. The survey found that Millennials invest about one-third of their funds in stocks and about the same amount in cash instruments. Another fear factor: the survey also found that about half of the Millennials were employed as opposed to two-thirds a decade ago. In perhaps the most telling number of the survey, 40% of Millennials agreed with the statement, "I will never feel comfortable investing in stocks."

7. **Under-banked.** Nearly half of Millennials are "under-banked," according to a study by Think Finance, and are choosing to use financial convenience products rather than traditional banking services. While most Millennials do have at least one traditional bank account, they are significantly more likely than other generations to use check cashing services, payday loans, and prepaid debit cards. As a result, they are utilizing services that are more expensive but faster and easier than traditional banking. Subjects in the study say they find traditional banking too time-consuming, inconvenient, and stressful.

8. **Growing up, financially.** According to the Transamerica Center for Retirement Studies, only about one-fifth of adult Millennials

have done any serious retirement planning, and 35% have no retirement plan. Most Millennials (73%) understand that they are not doing enough for their own retirements but that awareness hasn't created any urgency. And just over half (52%) agreed with the statement, "I prefer not to think about or concern myself with retirement investing until I get closer to my retirement date."

As Millennials become more "adult," their awareness of, and interest in, financial services will increase. Since most Millennials postpone adult milestones until their late 20s or early 30s, this current increased interest probably represents the vanguard, or oldest members, of the generation reaching that stage. That means that more than 60 million of their fellow Millennials will be discovering and entering this marketplace right behind them over the next decade or two, reshaping the industry.

FIFTEEN WAYS TO CONNECT WITH MILLENNIAL CLIENTS

1. **Get to the point.** Millennials are notoriously impatient. There is a lot of competition for their time and attention. Your opening should quickly and succinctly encapsulate what you can offer them. Consider the length of a typical text message, Facebook status update, or Twitter "tweet"—about 140 characters or less—and that will give you an idea of the bite-sized messages that Millennials like to digest. They believe everything should be that quick and easy.

   Try this: "This will take five minutes, max." (and make sure it does)

   Or a text: "Markets up again! Check it!"

2. **Up front.** Millennials are exposed to plenty of information online. If there is something wrong with what you are touting, they will probably discover it. Don't hide anything. Make sure all of the relevant information

you have is available to them. They will go online to look up what you tell them to see if it is true. Encourage it.

They will search your name on Google, Facebook, and Twitter to decide whether they like you. Embrace it. And, as with Generation X, beware of your online first impression—make sure it is something that would appeal to them.

> ·💡· **Try this:** "You can check all of this out at these major websites."

3. **Act your age.** Do not try to affect a young, quirky, or hip manner with Millennials, unless, of course, you *are* young, quirky, and hip. If someone is "trying too hard" to be young and "with it," Millennials will sense that, get turned off, and leave.

At the same time, communicate to them that you understand them and can help them get what they want. Genuine. Sincere. Helpful.

> ·💡· **Try this:** Be yourself, be natural, be straightforward.

4. **Freebies.** Every generation loves free stuff, and Millennials are no exception. Give them something for free, or close to free, if at all possible. Offer a free session or transaction. Enable them to access or try your product or service without financial obligation.

Millennials are attracted to the prospect of something for nothing, or at least a high level of flexibility and customization. Remember, this is a generation accustomed to buying just the song they want, not a whole album. Burger King's promise of "your way, right away" has always been the expectation for this generation.

> *Try this:* "Our new clients get a free subscription to this financial news service. It's a premium service that lets you track everything."
>
> *Or:* "This comes with free tax software that factors your investments into your taxes."
>
> *Or:* "We offer a few free services for the children of our clients who have been with us for a while."

5. **Latest technology.** Make sure your website is up-to-date, well-designed, and full of information that will help Millennials research and find your offerings and services.

   If possible, Millennial customers should be able to make transactions. If not, perhaps they can signal what they want or make an appointment via email, text, or instant message to meet with you. Offer free Wi-Fi in your office.

   > *Try this:* Set up a Twitter feed for your advisory (being cautious of industry regulations) and offer updates via text message.

   > *Or:* Post YouTube videos that teach the basic tenets of financial literacy and showcase your advisors.

6. **Self-esteem is everything.** Millennials were raised on self-esteem and value it above almost everything. Build rapport with Millennials by recognizing their individuality and accomplishments—build up their self-esteem. Admire them as individuals.

At the same time, be careful not to make any comments about appearance that may seem intrusive, judgmental, or inappropriate (in other words, "creepy"). Also, be careful about becoming too aware of the social media activity of clients, if you connect online. While Millennials tend to be fairly open with accepting online acquaintances, they still consider that a space for conversing with friends.

> *Try this:* "Tell me what I need to know about you." And remember what they've told you. Ask follow-up questions. Make notes. Let them talk; don't interrupt.
>
> *Or:* "I'm impressed by your (individual style, way they express themselves, level of knowledge on a topic, etc.)."
>
> *Or:* "I can see you're very concerned about the environment (or other social cause on their T-shirt). I admire your commitment."

7. **Guidance counseling.** Be a trusted guide who helps Millennial clients make a decision

that is good for them. Spend time with them and get to know them as individuals. Answer questions. Become a nonstressful resource who is going to help them get what they want.

There are many resources available for investment research and comparison, and Millennials will be looking at them. Get out in front of that process by suggesting the ones that are the most evenhanded or favorable to you. Let them know that they can text, email, or call you, without obligation, anytime they have a question or hear some confusing information.

> *Say:* "If you're interested, I'll be happy to walk you through this and show you how it works."
>
> *Or:* "I can show you some websites that have some great info on these funds."

8. **Control your reputation.** Manage your reputation among Millennials, especially online and in social media. Millennials are acutely aware of what others have and are doing. If

their peers have patronized your business, they are likely to be aware of their peers' experiences with you. They will share this information on social networks and other media with hundreds of friends. Again, get out in front of this process by acknowledging it. You might ask them if any of their friends have done business with you and if they were completely satisfied.

Millennials are more likely to share private information with one another. This generation regards personal information much differently than older generations. They share information more freely and may know the "nitty-gritty" details of their friends' business, so be ready to comment (or defend yourself).

> *Try this:* "Have any of your friends used our service? What did they like or dislike about it? I want to make sure we get everything just right here."

9. **Peer "pressure".** Peer testimonial is critical. Millennials frequently want to feel good about their decisions within their peer group. If you

have Millennial customers or employees that can attest to the quality of what you offer, bring those testimonials into your relationships with Millennials. Pass along snippets from texts, emails, and Facebook comments (with permission) from satisfied Millennial customers.

Millennials put great faith in peer-to-peer referrals. If you have some successful accounts with Millennials, ask them if they will speak to others about you. It could mean a lot.

> ⋅🔆⋅ **Try this:** "I know some folks in very similar situations to yours who worked with us and are very happy about it. I could put you in touch, and they could answer any questions you have about us."

10. **Common cause.** Millennials will be interested in firms or investments with altruistic aspects, such as environmental or social consciousness. They are the most likely to buy products or services that advertise their commitment to charitable or similar causes. If your firm supports any such organizations

or programs, make sure your Millennial customers are aware of it, even if it is just a recycling program.

Millennials want to know that they are making socially responsible investments and dealing with a socially responsible firm. It makes them feel better about themselves and is something that they will tout to their peers.

Try this: "These funds are only invested in sustainable enterprises."

Or: "Some of the income from this goes into relief efforts."

Or: "Our firm encourages our employees to mentor disadvantaged youth, and we offer one paid day per quarter for them to go do this volunteer work."

11. **Digital communication.** Millennials have distinct communication and technology preferences. They prefer text messages, instant messages, social networks, and email, pretty much in that order. They are not particularly fond of talking on the phone or going to

multiple meetings, both of which they find time consuming and intrusive. In addition to preferring digital communication, they expect text messages and emails to be acknowledged or answered instantly.

Effective communication with Millennials will involve some or all of these technologies. Technology is assumed and valued and is not feared. If you are entering a relationship with a Millennial, it is important to learn their preferred method of communication and to make it clear that you are comfortable with technology yourself. Do *not* overwhelm them with pushy or unwanted messages of any kind, which they regard as "spam" and a misuse of the technology they regard as their own.

> *Try this:* "What is the best way for me to contact you or update you? I'm pretty good with most of the technologies available, so I'll use what you prefer."

12. **Follow the herd.** Keep in mind that Millennials move in packs, so target them as a herd. If you

can get in front of a group of them, they'll likely think of you when choosing an advisor. Similarly, if you can identify popular Millennials—the leaders of the pack—winning them over will go a long way toward winning the approval of the group.

This mentality can also extend to online influencers. Pay attention to who the Millennials are paying attention to in your market and develop relationships with them. If these individuals are bloggers or promoters of any kind, expect to compensate them for access to their audience.

> *Try this:* "If I buy lunch for you and your buddies, would you invite them to join us for a quick tutorial? No sales, no pressure, no expectations— just education, so you'll be smarter investors."

13. **One of a kind.** This is the most individualistic generation; they are uniquely individualistic within their herds, odd as that may seem. They want what their friends have and want to do what their friends are doing, but they

want that to have a unique twist. In some cases, you may be able to offer something that is slightly customized, or you may be able to build a solution just for them.

Marketers and advertisers are already targeting Millennials with phrases such as "personally yours," "make it your own," and "as special as you are." Try to incorporate similar approaches into your relationships with Millennials.

> ☀ ***Try this:*** "I'm sure there are some things you feel strongly about that set you apart. Let's make my services work for you specifically"
>
> *Or:* "If we tweak this offer a little, you will have something really unique."

14. **Stay current.** Millennials tend to be most interested in what is current—what is hot or "viral" or has "buzz" right now. Make sure what you are offering is up to date and not yesterday's news. Even what would appear to other generations as fairly up-to-date can be labeled "sooo 5 minutes ago" by Millennials.

Technology promotes rapid changes and rapid awareness of those changes—and that awareness spreads among Millennials faster than any other generation.

> *Try this:* "These are some of the most innovative and exciting instruments on the market today..."

15. **Don't push it.** Millennials will not respond well to pressure, pushiness, or hard selling. Rather, you should continue to use the same approaches you used in engaging them and building a relationship with them.

    Millennials will not react well if your approach changes suddenly when it's time to make a decision. In other words, don't build your relationship with Millennials by honoring all of their preferences only to revert to pressure at the end of the process. This will have the feel of "bait and switch" to them.

> *Try this:* "Think about what we've discussed. Go over this material. Let's talk about this again in a few days."

Gen X, Millennials, and Social Media

While all generations use social media to some degree, Gen X and Millennials are much more likely to use it in making buying decisions. To these two generations, social media is both a toy and a tool. Through it, they get news, they get product suggestions from their peers, and they learn about products directly from manufacturers. Regardless of your personal beliefs around social media, your presence in the most popular social media of the day is vitally important to your practice. To Generation Xers and Millennials, social media today is the Yellow Pages of 30 years ago; you must be present to be "in the game."

As of this writing, the most prevalent social media platforms for business are LinkedIn, Facebook, and Twitter. While there are plenty of others, these three are consistently seen as relevant places for business knowledge to be shared.

This is not a book on social media—there are plenty of those available—but understanding how influential social media is when trying to reach Gen X and Millennial audiences is important.

These generations seek out information and will not buy what they don't understand. Furthermore, they will not buy from people they dislike. When determining whether to do business with you or not, they will enter your name into a browser search bar and see what comes up. More often than not, at the top of the list, will be your LinkedIn profile. (If you don't have a LinkedIn profile, get one now.) What does yours look like?

Most Baby Boomers will focus on their personal history in the business, designations, awards, and volunteer activities in their community. While there's nothing wrong with any of this content, it is not the best way for potential Gen X and Millennial clients to get to know you.

Your electronic first impression needs to get your prospective client excited to engage with you. Therefore, the content on your LinkedIn profile needs to not only discuss your past accomplishments but also how you serve your clients today and how you anticipate serving new clients in the future. Remember, Generation X and Millennials tend to be future focused. They want to know what will happen to them, not what you've done. So make sure your LinkedIn presence demonstrates how you are keeping up with new technologies and trends to help current and future clients achieve their goals.

The picture you select for yourself needs to be appropriate, too. While there is nothing wrong with a business headshot, adding something that shows a little of your character, of your flavor, of the real you may be nice. You want your Generation X and Millennial clients to see your photo, read your bio, and say to themselves, "I'd like to know this person," not just, "They appear qualified."

Put your name in several different search engines and see what comes up. Are you satisfied with what you see? How might you be able to change it?

While LinkedIn rules the business social media space, Facebook and Twitter are also vital. Take care to separate your personal and business accounts on both platforms. Many people use their personal Facebook pages to express opinions on politics, food, entertainment, and anything else. This is appropriate for friends, but may be detrimental to client relationships. Your business accounts should be professionally maintained, showing the same type of head shots discussed regarding the LinkedIn page, and posting regular items about business trends impacting your clients. You obviously can't discuss individual accounts, but you can discuss the forces influencing your collective clients' ability to save and prepare for retirement. Things like market trends, new mutual fund offerings, new occurrences around the office, or, simply, new hires that you want to feature on the page. To remain relevant on your Facebook page, you need to post new content at least three or four times a month. More than that is great but not too much more, or you become a nuisance to your Facebook users.

Twitter is a great platform for pointing others to information they may find interesting. Unless you're a noted expert in your field, bordering on a celebrity, your personal opinions, thoughts, and reflections are seldom what your Twitter users are going to want to read. A few times throughout the day as information strikes you as interesting or compelling is perfectly sufficient.

Many older advisors worry about having the additional time needed to manage a Facebook or a LinkedIn page. The truth is there is probably someone already on your staff, like a Millennial or Gen Xer, who would be delighted to take on this chore for you. They also know what is deemed important by their peers and will post salient content for you.

Five Key Advisor Questions for Preparing to Work with Millennials

Ask yourself:

1. What can I learn from the Millennials around me? Some of the easiest and least expensive research you can do is to watch your kids and their friends or other Millennials you may know or that work in your firm. Ask them why they buy what they buy, why they go where they go, and why they like what they like. Take note of your kids' shopping and buying habits and bring some of those ideas to your firm.

2. Should Millennials be part of my team? Millennials are very peer oriented, and it is worthwhile to have them as part of your team of advisors. They trust one another, they "click" with one another, and they tend want to do business with one another. But the Millennials are the newest generation in the workplace and are often risky new hires due to high turnover history. Hiring well, strong onboarding, and ongoing training are key.

3. Too much, too fast? Adjusting to appeal to this generation of 93 million people is certainly a smart decision, but be careful of going too far to accommodate them. It can look phony. Changing too much too fast may make Millennials look askance at you and may alienate the older generations that currently sustain you. Small, incremental, and nonrisky change is the best way to begin. Once started, build on it.

4. Should my meetings look or run differently when meeting with younger clients and prospects? The format of your client meetings may need to change as you engage your Millennial clients. More casual. More free flowing. A collared golf shirt versus a blazer. More beverage choices than simply coffee or a bottle of water. Lots more asking from you than telling by you. Lots of listening to anecdotes of what their friends are doing with their retirement planning and what they read most recently on the topic. Be an authority. Be confident. But there is no reason to be overly formal or

to demand that you're acknowledged as the only expert they need to listen to.

5. What is the message I project in how I conduct a new prospect meeting? Does the setting match what is important to a Millennial or to my traditional Boomer clients? Can I be comfortable and productive in a more social setting that would appeal to Millennials?

CHAPTER 6

THE GENERATIONAL TRANSITION

How to manage the transition of a practice built for Matures and Boomers into one that serves the Twitter and Snapchat generations is one challenge. Another is managing the transfer of the bulk of the wealth you are currently managing to a generation of heirs.

THE GREAT TRANSFER

John Havens and Paul Schervish from Boston College's Center on Wealth and Philanthropy report that the Baby Boomer generation in the U.S. is expected to pass $41 trillion to their heirs, largely the Millennials. However, over 80% of the inheritors of that wealth expect to use different financial advisors than the ones their parents used. That means that a huge amount of wealth will pass from one generation to another, but the financial advisors who worked hard to help build and transfer that wealth will be left out in the cold.

Reaching out to the next generation of clients is crucial to the survival and growth of any business. Now, more than ever, no business can assume that younger generations will make the same choices as their parents' and grandparents' generations. In fact, they probably won't.

An Existential Threat or Once-in-a-Lifetime Opportunity

Obviously, that poses a threat to an entire generation of advisors, but it also presents an enormous opportunity. One would expect the advisors to be actively developing relationships with future heirs, but most are doing very little to court the next generation. Why? Like most of us, financial advisors are more comfortable working with people like themselves, members of their own generation.

CASE STUDY: "MICHAEL AND JENNIFER"

Let's consider a pseudonymous but typical financial advisor, "Michael." Like the average financial advisor, he is a 53-year-old white male. His target market is people like him—about his age and with similar backgrounds. That's his "comfort zone." So when Michael thinks about new clients, he usually thinks about people like himself with whom he can easily connect. People who already have some assets built up in a retirement plan, and by collecting those assets, he will quickly begin earning income on them.

On the other hand, the children of Michael's clients, mostly Millennials, may seem alien to him. Consider one of them, a hypothetical 28-year old, "Jennifer." Michael is perfectly comfortable with her mom and dad, but she comes from a generational culture that is foreign to him, even if he has known her for a long time. She may have a tattoo somewhere and prefers texting to speaking to the person in front of her. Although Jennifer might be in line for an inheritance from her parents, the thought of trying to court her as a client so intimidates Michael that he'd rather pursue someone like himself as a new customer than someone who he already has a small relationship with, through her parents. He'll gladly take a cold call over a warm lead if the warm lead is someone who makes him uncomfortable.

Additionally, Jennifer has no assets of her own yet. She *might* get them *if* the parents' hopes for themselves go to plan. But there are many hurdles along the way: potential new taxes on retirement savings, rising costs of health care that may wipe out all of Jennifer's parents' savings, and the potential for new health-care technologies to keep Jennifer's parents alive for more years than their retirement calculator predicted. There is no guarantee that Jennifer will get the money. That's just what her parents hope will happen, and although they may have written all of this out, there are no guarantees.

So Michael sees Jennifer as a maybe. Additionally, he struggles to connect with her. The age gap makes connecting difficult. And the feeling of disconnection may be mutual. Jennifer may have rolled her eyes because Michael's firm doesn't recycle paper or offer free Wi-Fi in the lobby for clients or because Michael has awards and photos of himself all over the office. She will likely look for an advisor who shares her values when it's time to manage her inheritance.

It is human nature for Michael to gravitate toward like-minded people or to similar organizations. But diversifying outside his "comfort zone" has a big upside, if he's willing to do it.

There may still be time for Michael to connect with Jennifer's generation. But the consequences of ignoring the generational transition can come swiftly and at a real cost to his firm.

CASE STUDY: "DAVE"

Let's consider another hypothetical financial advisor "Dave." Dave, also a Baby Boomer in his 50s, lost a longtime friend and client to cancer. Dave had provided a valuable service for his friend, stewarding a 401(k) plan to a significant sum, complimenting his decisions in good times and holding his hand in bad. In return, the account had proved profitable for Dave's firm. When his client passed, Dave felt awful that his friend never had the chance to enjoy retirement, but all that was left to do was to follow through with the planned succession.

Once Dave handed over the last heir's inheritance, he knew it was the last he'd see of it. He watched as the results of a trusting twenty-five-year professional relationship walked out of his office, one heir at a time. "But that's my job, isn't it," Dave asked himself, "to pass on the money when the time comes?"

By the time Dave's client died, it was too late to do anything else. But could he have done something earlier in the relationship to cultivate relationships with the heirs, to connect with the next generation of clients? How do Baby Boomer advisors find common ground with a Millennial generation of heirs that communicates almost exclusively with its fingertips—through texting—and seems to show little of the traditional work ethic that made Dave and his clients so successful? In short, how does he make sure his clients' kids want him to be their financial advisor, too?

This process can be complex and requires sensitivity to both current and future generations of clients. See 12 Steps to Manage Generational Transition, page 163, for more tips in this area.

Case Study: "Jim and Earl"

Now let's look at an example of a firm taking these issues seriously. Baby Boomers Jim and Earl founded their firm in 1990 with six clients and about $5 million in assets to manage. Over two decades, they grew their business to more than one hundred clients and over $200 million of investments. Their primary source of growth? Word of mouth, the original peer-referral system. In a traditionally staid and discreet business, they let their work speak for itself in their close-knit community. The office door doesn't even bear the firm's name, and this approach worked well.

After 26 years, with retirement on the horizon, Earl and Jim are now looking to the future. Jamie and Chuck, both Gen Xers in their 40s, have joined the firm to help think about how to reach out to younger clients. How does a firm that has attracted clients predominantly via word of mouth brand itself for new generations? The leadership has given Jamie and Chuck the task of bridging the gap between long-standing and loyal current clients—Baby Boomers—while simultaneously targeting the next generations of clients—Generation X and the Millennials. The current clients likely prefer the discreet and traditional style of the firm. But the next generations respond more to websites, sponsorships, advertisements, social media, and the like.

Some suggestions for Jamie and Chuck:

First and foremost, the firm needs a new digital storefront in place of the old nameless front door.

Even with a word-of-mouth referral, younger generations will not beat a path to the firm's door. They'll head for a web browser instead. For prospective clients from younger generations, the firm's website is the new front door. The "about" and "bios" pages must show who the firm is and tell the partners' stories. History, recognition, and past accomplishments instill confidence for older generations, and these sections will do that. The firm's next generations of clients are looking for something different when they click though to the firm's site.

For Gen Xers and the Millennials, the website needs to show information about their own futures—where the firm can take them, rather than where the firm has been. Client testimonials from peers are a super way to showcase this, as is a sample questionnaire that the firm can put up on the site showing how they work with their clients to develop goals that are unique to each client.

Case studies are also helpful for attracting next-generation clients. Different from a testimonial, a case study should tell the story of how the firm customized its approach to meet a Millennial or Gen Xer's individual needs and situation. It should also highlight the reality of multiple financial commitments and demonstrate how the firm's approach has put the person on track to achieve his or her goals.

Approach the bio with a goal to showcase both professional aptitude and individual personality. Jamie and Chuck should consider an additional bio page or "the real me" section that gives clients and prospects a glimpse at advisors' lives outside of the office, including photos and comments reflecting family and hobbies. This tactic makes the advisor seem more human and approachable, creates potential for common ground, and makes the advisor look like a person potential clients may want to know. The balance of personal and professional is important, so they will want to avoid introducing controversial topics and bring in a professional photographer to take high-quality candids.

Jamie and Chuck should also propose a new video series addressing financial literacy needs. They can get their team to speak on camera about the different financial literacy needs that align with different stages of life. This will play into the way that Millennials like to "snack" on information rather than consume large whitepapers and reports. Examples might include: how to get the best rate for a mortgage, how to examine credit card offers, how to discover your own risk profile, the importance of investing for retirement over saving for retirement, when to become more cautious in your portfolio, and 529 plans vs. other savings tools for children's education.

If the firm has strong ties to a local or national nonprofit, they can showcase that on their website, too. Millennials, in particular, are an altruistic generation and will likely be interested in who a firm supports and why. Does the firm raise money for cancer research out of respect for a colleague who struggled with breast cancer or a client's child who is currently battling the disease? Tell that story somewhere on the site. Weave it into the fabric of the organization in an authentic way, and make it possible for clients to get involved via links to the organization's volunteer page or scheduled volunteer events with the firm staff. Jamie and Chuck can spearhead sharing these stories on social media, including photos of clients and advisors rolling up their sleeves and helping together. Without bragging, and by showcasing the non-profit's good works, they can make sure that clients and potential clients are aware of their altruistic efforts.

The depth of content on the website is important, too. It can't be a simple placeholder with contact information. Gen Xers and Millennials will use the website for extensive research and to establish a relationship with the firm before they contact a person. They will show up to meetings with an opinion based on the information they find on the firm's website ... and elsewhere on the web. To make sure that opinion supports their goals, Jamie and Chuck should rally their team to provide fresh perspectives that reflect the firm's position on routine and trending topics. They should also make it visually appealing through call-to-action buttons, images, and strong headlines. These features make the website easy to navigate, and information easy to find. The content must be there, but the design makes the first pitch.

A typical prospective client will look at something for three seconds to determine if they're interested in it, based mostly on the appeal of the design. If intrigued, they'll spend thirty seconds reading the big and bold text and scanning the rest. If what they see there looks good, they'll spend an additional three minutes reading the finer points. After that, they're gone.

In addition to strong perspectives, they should make the content visually appealing through call-to-action buttons, images, and strong headlines. These features make the website easy to navigate, and information easy to find. The content must be there, but the design makes the first pitch.

Finally, the firm's contact page should be updated to accommodate the different generations' preferences for different communication. For Millennials, that means more than a simple phone number and email address. Add mobile numbers for texting, Skype addresses, twitter handles, etc. as part of each advisor's bio and contact page.

These are just a few examples of advisors and clients, both in transition. How firms manage these challenges will determine whether they thrive, survive, or expire over the next few decades. One of our forthcoming publications will explore this massive professional transition and transfer of wealth—and what to do about it—in greater detail. For the time being, here is a look forward to a few of the steps we will be recommending and detailing to get your preparation started.

Twelve Steps to Manage Generational Transition

A robust online presence is the first prerequisite to attracting the next generation of clients. Numerous conversations with advisors who are struggling with these questions already, combined with years spent studying norms and habits across the generations, have yielded the following suggestions and best practices for shepherding your firm from one generation of clients to the next:

1. **Start with the parents.** Explain to your current clients that you'd like to help their children the same way you have helped them. With your clients' permission, get to know their children beyond names and birthdays. Reach out and introduce yourself. As they begin their transition into adulthood, try to set up a meeting with them in "neutral territory" like a coffee shop or restaurant. Pick up the phone, send an email, or text message them. You must be the one to initiate it.

2. **Plant a seed.** Plant the thought of being a multigenerational planner. Discuss the concept of getting to know all of their family tree. Where are they in the tree? Do they have parents? Brothers and sisters? Children? Nephews and nieces? Work toward building trust with your new client, so they'll be open to introducing you to other members of their family tree.

3. **Strengthen the relationship.** Before you extend your relationship with other family members, make sure you have a solid relationship with your current clients, including both members of a couple. Many times an advisor may have the majority of dealings with one spouse, yet be representing the couple as a whole. This can cause problems upon the death of the person with whom you have the primary relationship. Make efforts to involve both spouses equally so that you can continue to serve as a trusted advisor in any situation. That trust will help open doors to other family members, but it needs to be solid with your initial clients first.

4. **Acknowledge clients' children.** Recognize important life events in the lives of your clients' children such as birthdays, graduations, and awards.

5. **Lend a hand when you can.** Use your network to support the goals of clients' children. For example, if you know alumni of a

school a clients' child wishes to attend, offer to introduce them.

6. **Be a family firm.** Many successful advisors offer annual family events like a summer picnic or a year-end holiday movie where clients are asked to invite children and grand-children to the event.

7. **Find out what they know.** Gauge the financial literacy of clients' children or younger refer-rals by asking what financial decisions their friends are making. Millennials share lots of personal information with one another. They know what their friends are up to. More importantly, you'll get a sense of their finan-cial acumen as you listen.

8. **Teach and explain.** Teach clients' children what you do. Ask your clients if you can use their own scenario as an example for their children. Say to the kids, "The easiest way for you to understand what I do is to tell you how I work with your parents and what it means for you." No need to share account

information, just describe the services you offer and how you are paid from them. You're teaching here.

9. **Be a resource.** Consider offering educational seminars for clients' children on "Dealing with Money." Upon college graduation, gift a client's child a copy of *Networking for College Students (and Recent Graduates): Nonstop Business Networking That Will Change Your Life* by Andrea Nierenberg and offer to meet with them to offer some networking tips.

10. **Put the focus on them, not you.** Ask the children to talk about what they want for their own future, not what their parents or others want for them. Youth are future focused. Don't dwell on your background. This is about their future, not your past.

11. **Offer guidance.** Offer insight into their financial options. Don't lecture from the position of an expert; teach from the position of a friend. Point out the opportunities as well as the hazards. Offer your advice should they

ever need it. Be clear that you'll advise them based on their own situation, not act as a surrogate for their parents. Offer to help their friends, if ever needed. Tell them that they can come to see you together if they want, since Millennials like to move in packs.

12. **Invest in the future.** Recognize that developing relationships with next-generation clients may be an investment in the future. Many firms have lower payouts on smaller accounts. Nonetheless, next-generation relationships are important to nurture to grow your practice in the future.

CONCLUSION

SELLING HAS CHANGED. Client relationships have become more complex. Your traditional patterns of client behavior and account lifecycles are no longer reliable. Or maybe nothing has changed.

This book conveys the changing demographics and shifting experiences that are giving many financial advisors anxiety they haven't felt since the Great Recession. But it also shares a path forward.

The different generations in the marketplace today are, indeed, different. They are different than each other, and they are different than prior generations were at the same stages and ages. Yet they are still people.

Luckily, your livelihood rests not in predicting their behavior, but with connecting with them as individuals, building relationships, understanding their needs, and showing them how to get there. Nothing has changed about what you need to do.

The difference is in who you are making those connections with (typically those younger than you, perhaps for the first time in your career), how you build those relationships (online and with a faster pace), when you demonstrate your understanding (before you even meet them), and how you show them the way (with lots of transparency, buy-in, and options).

The pressure is on to connect with the next generation—especially those Millennials poised to inherit significant wealth in the years to come—and the financial advisors who are savvy enough to find fun in that challenge rather than fearing the unknown will be the ones to jump ahead.

About the Author

CAM MARSTON is the leading expert on generational change and its impact on the marketplace. As an author, columnist, blogger, and lecturer, he imparts a clear understanding of how generational demographics are changing the landscape of business. Marston and his firm, Generational Insights, have provided research and consultation on generational issues to hundreds of companies and professional groups, ranging from small businesses to multinational corporations, as well as major professional associations, for over 20 years.

Marston's books, articles, columns, and blog describe and analyze the major generations of our time: Matures (born before 1946), Baby Boomers, (born 1946–1964), Generation X (born 1965–1979), and Millennials (born 1980–2000). He explains how their generational characteristics and differences affect every aspect of business, including recruiting and retention, management and motivation, and sales and marketing.

His first book, *Motivating the "What's in It for Me?" Workforce* (2005), explores the characteristics and motivations that each generation brings to the workforce, and suggests management tactics applicable to any business setting. His second book, *Generational Insights* (2010), is a guide to the best practices in managing generational issues. *Generational Selling Tactics That Work* (2011) is the first book-length study of generational approaches to sales and marketing. His two training videos have been best sellers since introduced in 2005. Marston's expertise has also been featured in the *Wall Street Journal, The Economist,* the *Chicago Tribune, BusinessWeek, Fortune, Money,* and *Forbes,* as well as on *Good Morning America, CNN International,* and *BBC News.* He writes columns for *Investment Advisor, CNBC,* and *Investment News,* and has been a featured columnist in *AdvisorOne Magazine, ThinkAdvisor,* and *Fast Company* among others. His blog at generationalinsights.com tracks the latest changes and developments in generational issues and demographics.

As a consultant, Marston has provided insight and advice to leadership at the nation's most prominent corporations and multinational corporations including American Express, Fidelity, BASF, Nestle, Schlumberger, Merrill Lynch, Kellogg, Coca-Cola, Macy's, Warner Brothers, ESPN, Qualcomm, RE/MAX, and Eli Lilly. He has also offered presentations and consultations for the U.S. Department of Agriculture, the Internal Revenue Service, and the U.S. Army, as well as major professional associations such as the American Bankers Association, the Financial Services Roundtable, and the Million Dollar Roundtable. He is an ongoing instructor at Belmont University's Scarlett School of Leadership.

Marston's insights and expertise are the product of research and consultation across a wide range of industries as well as his own early-career background in corporate sales and research. He holds a Bachelor of Arts from Tulane University. He is a native and resident of Mobile, Alabama.

Resources

Cam Marston, *Generational Insights—Practical Solutions for Understanding and Engaging a Generationally Disconnected Workforce* (2010).

Cam Marston, *Generational Selling Tactics that Work: Quick and Dirty Secrets for Selling to Any Age Group* (2011, Wiley).

Cam Marston, *How to Train Millennials* (2012, Kindle Download).

Cam Marston, *Motivating the "What's In It For Me?" Workforce: Manage Across the Generational Divide and Increase Profits* (2007, Wiley).

David K. Foot, *Boom, Bust & Echo: Profiting from the Demographic Shift in the 21st Century* (2001). David Foot's book examines demographic change, and how it relates to business opportunities. While focusing mostly on Canadian data, the general *life-cycle* model of analysis can easily be applied to U.S. generational change.

Employee Benefit Research Institute (www.ebri.org) The EBRI publishes results of its annual *Retirement Confidence Survey*, which measures Americans' confidence in their ability to retire financially secure.

Pew Research Center (www.pewsocialtrends.org) Pew regularly publishes studies which analyze generational change.

Transamerica Center for Retirement Studies (www.trans americacenter.org/retirement-research/) Transamerica conducts an annual survey of a large, representative number of American workers, and publishes the results broken down by generation, gender, education and incomes of these workers.